SALES
Don't Just
HAPPEN

Also by Stephan Schiffman

Getting to "Closed"

Cold Calling Techniques (That Really Work)

Make It Happen Before Lunch

High Efficiency Selling

The Consultant's Handbook

The 25 Sales Habits of Highly Successful Salespeople

SALES
Don't Just
HAPPEN

26 PROVEN STRATEGIES TO
INCREASE SALES IN ANY MARKET

STEPHAN SCHIFFMAN

Dearborn™
Trade Publishing
A **Kaplan Professional** Company

This publication is designed to provide accurate and authoritative information in regard to the subject matter covered. It is sold with the understanding that the publisher is not engaged in rendering legal, accounting, or other
professional service. If legal advice or other expert assistance is required, the
services of a competent professional should be sought.

Editorial Director: Donald J. Hull
Acquisitions Editor: Mary B. Good
Senior Project Editor: Trey Thoelcke
Interior Design: Lucy Jenkins
Cover Design: Scott Rattray
Typesetting: Elizabeth Pitts

© 2002 by Stephen Schiffman

Published by Dearborn Trade Publishing, a Kaplan Professional Company

Printed in the United States of America

03 04 10 9 8 7 6 5 4 3

Library of Congress Cataloging-in-Publication Data

Schiffman, Stephan.
    Sales don't just happen : 26 proven strategies to increase sales in any mar-
ket / Stephan Schiffman.
        p.   cm.
Includes index.
    ISBN 0-7931-5463-4
    1. Selling. 2. Strategic planning. 3. Success in business.   I. Title.
    HF5438.25 .S3346 2002
    658.8'1—dc21

                                                        2002006509

Dearborn Trade books are available at special quantity discounts to use for
sales promotions, employee premiums, or educational purposes. Please call
our special sales department, to order or for more information, at 800-621-
9621, ext. 4307, or write to Dearborn Trade Publishing, 30 South Wacker Drive,
Suite 2500, Chicago, IL 60606-7481.

To SHS

C O N T E N T S

A C K N O W L E D G M E N T S

One of the things I've all learned over the years is that most salespeople simply let things happen. They don't *make* things happen, don't concentrate on moving the sales process forward. By that I mean advancing it consistently toward the point where the buyer actually decides to purchase and use the product or service. To me, sales are relatively simple. They require us to initiate conversations about how to help people do what they do better; then we transfer that information into reasonable proposals that ultimately will make sense to the prospect. If we do our job, the prospect then becomes a customer, someone who uses what we sell. While this process sounds simple, the reality of turning any idea into a mutually beneficial reality can, of course, be quite a challenge. Learning to overcome that challenge is what this book is all about.

The writing of a book is a complicated process, one not done in a vacuum. Over the course of my 27 years of training salespeople in North America, Europe, and the Pacific Rim, it has been my privilege to have the best support network in the world.

I would like to thank a number of people for helping to make this book a reality, beginning with Brandon Toropov, who has worked with me for the last 15 years on a variety of projects. Brandon is the senior writer for our training company, but he's more than that; he has become a personal friend. Brandon is the kind of person you meet and then wonder just where all the intelligence and the wisdom have originated. In the years that I have known him I have seen him write, direct, and produce a variety of projects—not simply sales training books. Brandon is a unique talent in his own right, and I thank him for his contribution to this book.

Equally important is the support that we get in the work that we do at D.E.I. Management Group. Tina Bradshaw has been with us for five years and has done an extraordinary job in scheduling. Carlos Alvarez works diligently to make sure that the company's billing is done properly. Alan Koval handles the accounting department, and Surendra Sewsankar does a yeoman's job in balancing the variety of tasks he is assigned. In the distribution department, David Rivera ensures that all our material gets to the right place at the right time. And of course, there's our creative services department, led by Fredrik Rydlun. Together with Scott Forman and Brandon, Fredrik helps to rewrite and recraft the ideas in our face-to-face training programs for audiences in a variety of media.

My administrative assistant, Martha Rios is without peer, as are Lesha Connell and Anganie Ali; their work and help with sales and office matters are greatly appreciated.

As a training company, we all work together to conduct nearly 2,000 events in a year, and the results are incredible. We have had literally thousands of salespeople comment positively on the effectiveness of our programs, and on the ease of im- plementing our fundamental selling concepts into their daily routine.

I must take the opportunity to thank the people at Dearborn, who have shown truly extraordinary commitment to this project. These include Mary Good, Leslie Banks, Terri Joseph, and Trey

Thoelcke, whose patience once again knew no bounds. My gratitude also goes out to Stephanie Kip Rostan and Daniel Greenberg at James Levine Communications.

I would be remiss if I did not credit the people who have supported D.E.I. most over the years. This group includes our Executive Vice President for sales, Lynne Einleger, who's been with us for 15 years and has lead the sales force with professionalism by her example. Our Executive Vice President, Steven J. Bookbinder, (15 years) conducts our programs as a true professional. He is an example of someone whose dedication shows no bounds. Our Vice President, Michele Reisner, (16 years) began the process of developing the material of speech into the material of word. Also in this group are the senior members of our extraordinary sales force, specifically: George Richardson, Vice President Stacia Skinner, and Vice President Gino Sette. Just as worthy of gratitude are the disciples whose full-time job it is to take the message out to the world at large—our trainers. These are the people who travel each and every day to make sure that the programs are delivered effectively. They include Vice President Raul Nunez, whose 6 years of travel and training is noted, Andrew Daino (five years), and Arturo Jackson (2 years).

I must express my gratitude, for the last 30 years, to an extraordinary and truly special woman. I thank Anne for her patience, understanding, support and love. Thank you, too, to Daniele and Jennifer, whose youthful enthusiasm has turned into mature understanding.

At this point, there are over a million copies of my books in print, which means that they have reached at least that many salespeople. Accordingly, I extend my last "thank you" to you. If you're a salesperson or a sales manager, you are the engine that drives the world economy. You do that by beginning each new day with the desire to succeed. We all owe you a debt of thanks.

INTRODUCTION

*A*bout a year ago, I was talking to a senior member of my company's management team about an opportunity with a Fortune 500 firm. I said, "What's up? When are you talking with them next?"

He said, "I'm on top of it. I'm supposed to call them in December."

I said, "You're on top of it? Have you checked the calendar? It's October. What are you telling me? Are you telling me that you're planning on leaving this relationship alone for the next two months, just because they told you you should call back in December?"

He said, "Uh, well, gee, hmmm . . ."

At that point, I picked up a pair of boxing gloves I keep next to my desk for just such an occasion. I flung the boxing gloves in his direction and said, "Go get 'em, Rocky! Make some noise in the ring for me, okay? Find some reason to get us on their calendar between now and the end of the month. Go!"

He took the boxing gloves to his office, then tried to call our contact that morning. As a result, he learned a couple of interesting things. First, our contact had been laid off. Second, the company was undergoing some major structural changes and wouldn't be working with us for the foreseeable future.

Here's my question to you: If he hadn't made that call, and if he'd spent three weeks putting together a killer proposal to pass along to our contact when he made the call in December, how smart would that have been?

You need a certain number of "no" answers to generate a yes answer... but you must also avoid wasting too much of your time on no answers that sound like yes answers.

As it stood, we were actually looking at an old-fashioned "no" answer. I'm in sales, so that doesn't really bother me. What bothers me is being on the fence with anyone. If I'm on the fence with someone, I always feel like I have to assume that one of us has really gotten off the fence, and just hasn't gotten around to telling the other person yet.

It's actually good to accumulate "no" answers as long as we recognize them for what they are. That's because it takes a certain number of no answers to generate a single "yes" answer. Now, it would certainly be nice if the only time you ever had to deal with "no" was when the person actually said to you, "No, don't call us for a while."

The truth is, though, that if you make it a habit to wait for someone to say, "No, we're not interested!" or something similar, you may spend too much of your time waiting. Fortunately, there's a much better definition of no and the yes in sales. To be effective as a salesperson, you must learn to hear yes when people agree to a Next Step with you. And you must learn to hear no when people refuse to give you the kind of specific commitment to short-term action that involves a date and time. We call such a commitment a Next Step. And at my company, if you're working with us and we don't have a short-term commitment for a Next Step from you, we want to know how we can get that Next Step from you.

Here's how we look at Next Steps. If any of the things people say to us while we're talking on the phone or meeting with them in person results in no Next Step, we have to translate that response in exactly the same way we would if we were to hear the word no.

Think of it this way: Some people do buy from us. Some people don't buy from us. Most of the people who do buy from us follow a predictable pattern. They give us a Next Step!

So we have to start looking for that pattern. And we have to start thinking about ways to make that pattern more likely to come about.

This book is all about making Next Steps happen. It's about making noise in the sales cycle. I've tried to make sure it's direct, concise, and full of information you can actually use. I'd love to hear what you think about what shows up between these covers, because it's basically the distillation of about 30 years of sales and marketing experience. So please get in touch with me at contactus@dei-sales.com to let me know what you thought of *Sales Don't Just Happen.*

Are you ready to make some noise?

CHAPTER 1

...in which we learn the difference between selling and order taking

"The doer alone is the one who learns."

—*FRIEDRICH NIETZSCHE*

*S*ales don't just happen.

Orders happen, of course. Someone calls us up and says, "Do you sell this stuff I'm looking for? Oh, you do? Great. Can I get some?" We take down the details. We fill the order.

But that's not selling. That's taking orders.

In order for a sale to happen, we have to do something deliberate and impossible to ignore—something that all but forces the other person to respond to us. The people who then do respond to us are, by definition, our prospects; they're the ones on which we should focus our attention.

At our company, whenever we talk about a prospect, we're

talking about someone who has demonstrated by action

that he or she is willing to discuss the possibility of using
our products and services. This person is moving through
the steps of the sales process with us.

FROM THE FRONT LINES

"Dear Mr. Schiffman: . . . Please take the time to read the following, as I truly want you to realize the effect you have had on my career. First, my wife, my two young children, and [I] would like to say thank you. . . . In August of 1999, [I decided] to pursue a career in sales. . . . I accepted [an] entry level offer and I started on February 14, 2000. After the first day, I almost quit . . . . People were hanging up on me left and right. A young sales rep approached me and told me I was talking too much and saying the wrong things [and gave me one of your tapes]. . . . On March 11, 2001, my business changed. I had a bad day on the road and I was 45 minutes from the office. I popped in your tape and it was like magic—all of a sudden everything started to become clear. . . . Since then, I have purchased all of your books and tapes and particularly the book on closing had tremendous effect on my business. . . . Last Monday, I was promoted to Branch Manager of our Northeast Sales Course in Nashville, New Hampshire. . . . I don't believe I would be in this position today if it were not for that day in March when I first listened to you. . . . I don't know what else to say, but thank you from the bottom of my heart. I will continue to introduce you to every new salesperson I come in contact with. . . . Thank you again for the opportunity to have a life-changing effect on my family."

—A sales manager in New Hampshire

I'm not very big on boasting, but I have to admit that I'm proud to receive letters like the one you just read. I'm also proud to be able to say that I get them regularly—usually three or four letters like this every week, from all over the world.

Would you be interested to learn what it is that inspires all those letters?

In essence, it's a single, simple principle. Believe it or not, one idea makes success stories like the one you just read possible.

One idea. And that one idea is what this book is all about.

One central concept supports and inspires everything we train at my company, D.E.I. Management Group. We specialize in helping people get that one basic idea. That's what we do.

Please note that getting the idea is not the same as simply hearing it. Salespeople hear this idea all the time.

Hearing or reading a good idea is wonderful—it's a first step—but it's not enough to ensure success.

I've noticed that when salespeople get the idea—perhaps after reading it in a book, listening to one of my tapes, or after we've repeated the idea to them in various forms during training—their whole body language changes. And so does their way of describing what they do for a living. They say things like:

- "It was like magic."

- "Everything became clear."

- "All of the sudden, I understood what I was supposed to be doing."

So what do we know so far? We know that selling comes down to a single, powerful idea—one idea that has a remarkable way of changing your career once you get it.

When I explain this single, simple idea to people who don't sell for a living, I sometimes hear, "That's so obvious!" I agree. It is obvious. It's so obvious that it's very easy to ignore. In fact, it's so obvious that it's incredibly easy—probably too easy—to hear this idea without getting it. Getting it means being motivated enough to put it into action.

But that's the way it is with this idea. People hear it, see it in action, or read it on the page and say to themselves, "Yes, that makes sense. That's certainly true. Now, what else have you got for me?"

And when they say that, they miss the chance to get the concept—an opportunity to completely transform their own career. They don't realize that they've already learned, or at least heard, what they now ought to put into practice.

Think again of the quote with which we began this chapter: "The doer alone is the one who learns."

Perhaps you're thinking, "Okay, so what do I do?"

You already know. Or at least you already should.

The idea I'm talking about isn't complex. You don't need a computer, or a special Web site, or a degree in business to understand this idea or put it into practice. As I've said, it's one (seemingly) obvious, simple lesson—a lesson with a thousand implications that somehow eludes the vast majority of salespeople. In fact, the lesson I'm talking about appears over and over again in this book. I've built it into every chapter—including this one.

Yes, that means what you think it means. I have already expressed this single, career-changing idea in this very chapter.

Did it slip past you unnoticed?

Once you get this concept, your whole career will swing into a new direction like the point of a magnetized compass needle. You'll know exactly where true north is, and you'll understand what you're really supposed to do as a salesperson. You will eventually find that you can hardly help putting this idea into action, regardless of the business situation in which you find yourself.

POINTS TO PONDER

- Once you really get the idea this book is built around, you'll start making positive changes in your selling routine almost without meaning to, almost without noticing the principle you're putting into action.

- Once you get this critical foundation concept, you'll wonder how it could possibly have floated past you undetected the first ten, or fifty, or one hundred times you heard it.

- Again: If you've read this far in the book, you've already encountered the one simple idea that can completely transform your career. It's not hidden. It's not complicated. It's right here. And it's waiting for you to take action.

Did you see it?
Did you get it?

CHAPTER 2

...in which we find out who's really playing ball with us

"I don't know the key to success, but the key to failure is trying to please everybody."

—BILL COSBY

Some people say they're salespeople, but really aren't. You can tell they're not really salespeople, because it's obvious that every business relationship they're working on is as important as every *other* business relationship they're working on.

No successful salesperson, in my experience, works that way.

Sales is a matter of throwing out a ball to a lot of different people—and following up effectively with those people who throw the ball back.

What do I mean by "throwing out the ball"?

If you were in one of my training sessions, I might toss a small foam ball in your direction. In doing that, I'm eliciting some kind of response from you. Will you catch the ball or will you let it fall to the floor? Will you try to catch it and miss it? Will you throw it back?

The same thing happens when I ask you a question during a training program. You have to do something in response. Even staring at me silently is some kind of a response to a question. I've learned something about you by your decision not to say anything.

"Throwing out the ball" means doing something deliberate and impossible to ignore—something that all but forces the other person to *respond* to us in some way. The people who then *do* throw the ball back to us are, I would argue, in a very special category.

The people who answer our question, or respond to our suggestion, or otherwise throw the ball back to us have *demonstrated* that they're willing to dedicate their time, energy, and attention *right* now to exploring the possibility of working with us. That's worth noticing! We should make those people our first priority!

What's the alternative?

Assuming that every business relationship we're working with is just as important as every other business relationship we're working on. *And that's absurd.*

Again: This is a distinction that seems obvious, but many of the "salespeople" I work with don't put it into practice.

Imagine that, when you make cold calls or do anything else to get someone interested in what you sell, you're throwing a ball. And imagine that, every time you dial someone's number and hear someone say hello, what you're really doing is throwing out a ball and saying, "I'm looking for someone who's willing to play ball with me." What will happen in response?

FROM THE FRONT LINES

Recently, during one of our lunchtime sales meetings, I asked one of our new salespeople, "How many new first appointments did you set today?"

She said, "One." (That's her quota—one new appointment a day. If she doesn't set one new appointment a day, she hears about it from her manager.)

I said, "Great. When are you meeting with this person?"

She said, "Well, I'm not actually meeting with him face to face. We've set up a conference call."

I said, "Then the total number of new appointments you set today was *zero*. You haven't hit your quota for the day. Get back on the phone and keep dialing until you schedule a first meeting with somebody else, and don't leave the office until you've scheduled that meeting."

That may seem harsh. But was it really?

A face-to-face meeting is a clear signal that someone is playing ball with you. The person is willing to set aside time in his or her schedule, stop everything that's going on during the day, and meet with you in person. In my experience, scheduling a first phone appointment is just not as clear a signal of interest as scheduling a first sit-down meeting.

In order to sell effectively (which is different from simply taking orders), we have to take action to make sales happen. We have to take action in a manner that cannot be ignored and that prompts some kind of response from the person with whom we're trying to connect. If we do this, and monitor the responses we get, we will always know who's playing ball with us and who isn't.

We'll say, "Why don't you and I get together to talk about this next Tuesday at 2:00?" Then we'll get some kind of response. Maybe that response will be positive. Maybe it will be negative.

After we've concluded our discussion with this person, dealt with any initial negative responses, and asked again for the Next Step, we'll have to ask ourselves a tough question: Do I really have a Next Step with this person? Has this person cleared a specific slot in the calendar to sit down with me and talk about the possibility of working together?

No?

Then that person is not playing ball with us. That's good to know if we're trying to figure out whether we've hit our daily target of one appointment per day with someone new.

When I get stuck in that conference call trap, you know what I do? As the call begins, I ask a few very basic questions, find out what the people at that company are doing, and then say, "You know what? Based on what you've told me, you and I really ought to get together. What are you doing next Monday at 10:00?"

In doing that, I throw out the ball. Will the person catch it and throw it back? Catch it and stare at it? Let it fall to the floor?

Something interesting is going to happen when I ask that question. But it won't happen *unless* I throw out the ball.

Again: *We have to take action to make sales happen.*

When I teach people how to make cold calls, I make sure that they don't say things like, "Can we set up a meeting?" or "Could we get together sometime next week?" These questions beat around the bush and point the call in a direction we really don't want to go. What I teach people to say is, "I'd like to come in and meet with you. Could we get together Tuesday at 2:00?"

Suddenly, we're not talking about whether we've got a face-to-face appointment with the contact, but when that appointment is going to take place.(Setting first appointments by phone is, in my experience, a critical sales skill for field salespeople. Those who don't learn how to do so effectively, and don't hit daily first appointment (FA) quotas, rarely succeed over the long term. For more information, see Appendix A, Seventeen Keys to Getting More Appointments.)

Selling is the art of producing tension as a means of identifying who is really moving from step to step through the sales process with you. That tension doesn't come about on its own. You have to generate it. You have to be willing to engage in what I call *making noise.*

> *Selling requires you to produce creative tension in a given business relationship. If you don't produce creative tension, the person you're talking to falls back into his or her usual way of doing things, and that probably doesn't include working with you.*

Mind you, I'm not talking about making prospects tense. I am talking about generating a *healthy* tension within the business relationship, the kind of tension that lets you know exactly where you stand.

Again: What's the alternative?

You're trying to start a game of catch. How are you doing this? By sitting quietly on the pitcher's mound of a baseball diamond holding a ball in your hand as dozens of people walk by while you wait for someone to say, "Gee, I just read your mind. What a great idea. Let's play catch."?

You might be waiting there for a while.

There's a line in a Bob Dylan song that goes something like this: "This should get interesting any minute now." That's kind of the philosophy behind what we teach people to do. Throw out a ball and change the status quo—shake it up—in any number of different ways. Whenever we take the initiative to do that, we *know* for certain that, one way or another, things will start to get interesting *right now.*

Sales don't just happen.

When we take the initiative and produce some (appropriate) tension-inspiring activity in the business world, we prompt a reaction of some kind from the person with whom we're dealing. The *reaction* we get tells us *who is* and *who is not* playing ball with us.

"Throwing out the ball" is the correct metaphor for what we're talking about here because it's an *unignorable* act. When you throw out a ball in someone's direction, you will know, in short order, whether or not the person wants to play catch with you!

This process of making noise is the best possible strategy for moving through the steps of the process with a given person. When you do something that's impossible to ignore, and when you monitor the response you get back, you know, instantly, who is playing catch with you and who isn't. You know who's moving through the selling process with you.

POINTS TO PONDER

- In order to sell, we have to challenge the status quo— what is already happening in the person's life. The status quo—not any single organization, company, or individual—is our true competition. The status quo—*what the other person is doing right now*—is what we are really competing against.

- The status quo is what really makes sense to a prospect. Around my office, we call the ongoing process of challenging the status quo in a way that's impossible to ignore *making noise.*

- *Making noise* means doing something that requires a response.

- *Making noise* means finding out whether someone is really playing ball with you.

- *Making noise* means accepting the person's suggestion of a conference call, joining the call, asking the questions you need to ask, and then saying, "You know what, this call has convinced me that we really ought to get together and talk about this in person. Why don't I come by your office Monday at 10:00?"

- We want the other person to conclude that it makes sense to buy from us. In order to get to that point, though, we must propose a lot of other steps and see whether those make sense.

- In a way, our job as salespeople is to come up with steps that could make sense, and keep proposing them until we find something that does.

CHAPTER 3

... in which we learn about the steps of the sales process

"Define your business goals in such a way that others can see them as you do."

—GEORGE F. BURNS

In Chapter 2, I mentioned "the steps of the sales process." What does that mean?

There are really only four steps to any sale. Look at these four boxes.

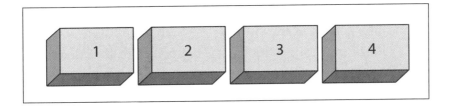

Assume, for a moment, that there are, in fact, four steps to the sales process. What *must* be the objective of the very first step?

When I ask that question during my sales training seminars I receive many different answers. Some people tell me, "The objective of the first step is to establish rapport." Some people say, "The objective of the first step is to learn what the prospect needs." And others say, "The objective of the first step is to begin to get to know what makes the other person tick, and identify his or her personality style."

All of those answers are convincing and intelligent—and all of them are dead wrong. The objective of the first step of the sales process is in fact nothing more or less than getting to the second step of the sales process.

If someone isn't moving through the steps of the sales process with you, that person is not "playing ball." That person is not, by my definition of the word, a prospect.

So when we talk about selling, what we're really talking about is making noise throughout the sales process in a way that asks a thousand variations on a single, impossible-to-ignore question: Are you ready to play ball with me?

That's the key principle. If the person isn't moving through the steps with you, you've got nothing.

Let me explain what's happening in each of those four steps of the sales process.

We'll begin with the most obvious step, which is the one on the far right. If it's a selling a process, somebody has to be buying something, so the step on the right-hand side is the decision to buy, also known as the close.

A lot of interesting things can happen after that decision, including the decision to start the whole process over and buy

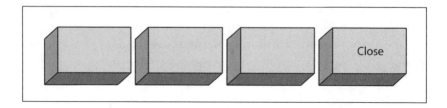

from you again. Truth be told, I'd much prefer to think of this entire process as a buying process rather than a selling process. Most sales professionals and sales managers, though, are used to thinking of it as a selling or closing process, so I'll use that terminology.

The box on the far right-hand side represents a decision by the customer to buy from us. In the standard sales jargon, we consider that sale to be closed. So that's the fourth step of the process. Actually, there isn't a final step, because our objective is to work with this person for the foreseeable future—not just today. Our real objective in sales is not to close the deal, but to get people to use our product or service, preferably forever. In order to do that, we have to look at matters from the other person's point of view and suggest something that actually makes sense to him or her. That's the decision we're describing in that fourth box.

Now then: What's the preliminary step that makes that decision possible? We call the third step the proposal or plan step. That's the point at which we make a recommendation or submit a plan that we trust is going to make enough sense to the prospect for him or her to actually use what we have to offer.

How do we know that what we're recommending will make sense? Well, we don't unless we've gathered the right information. This brings us to the second step of the sales process, the information-gathering or interviewing step.

This is probably the most critical step of them all; it's also the step salespeople are most likely to rush through or skip over entirely.

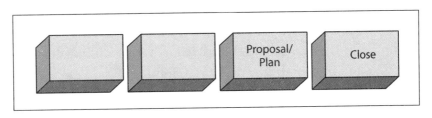

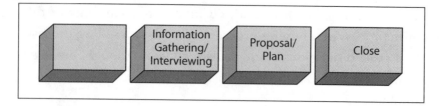

Our definition of effective selling is asking people what they do, how they do it, where they do it, when they do it, with whom they do it, and why they do it that way. Then, and only then, do we ask how we can help them do it better. The key word there is do, and it is during the information-gathering phase that we learn about this do—which may have no connection whatsoever with what we assume the prospect needs.

Before that step comes the opening or qualifying step; this is equivalent to the first contact or appointment. You can't just walk in the door and start firing off questions. You have to do something to open up the relationship. In our industry, sales training, this initial phase typically takes place as a result of a cold call from one of our salespeople to someone who has not yet heard of us or thought about working with us. When salespeople have scheduled a first face-to-face appointment with a prospect, we regard them as being at this first step.

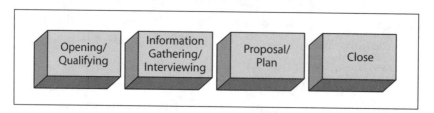

Notice: You can't move through these cycles on your own! You have to be working with the prospect at each step. Think about it. If the person doesn't agree to meet with you, you've got nothing. If the person agrees to meet with you but doesn't give you any information, you've got nothing. If you get all the right information but you present the plan to someone who has no power to make decisions, you've got nothing.

Sales don't just happen. You have to initiate forward movement with the right person and see what happens next. You have to make sure that both you and the prospect know where you are in the selling process at all times. You have to be sure that you both think it's a good idea to move forward from one step to the next. In my experience, the only way to pull that off is by focusing the sale on what the other person does and by constantly making it clear to the prospect, in a way that's absolutely impossible to ignore, what you plan to do next with him or her.

Sometimes people ask me, "You mean I have to say what I want to do next—out loud? Suppose what I plan to do next is totally wrong for this person?" Well, if what you plan to do next is totally wrong, wouldn't you like to know that before you spend any of your time doing it?

Here's the paradox of selling. When you find out that you're on the wrong track, that's great! You now have more information than you did before . . . and you've saved yourself a lot of time. When you reach a dead end, thank your lucky stars. You don't have to waste any more time preparing things for that inactive lead. You can focus on relationships that actually are moving forward, or that could move forward, rather than focus on ones that you know aren't moving forward.

If you're a salesperson, you must make sure that every step you're taking in a business relationship is with someone who's really playing ball with you. What does that mean? It means you must make absolutely sure that you're moving through the steps of the sales process with the full, engaged, aware participation of the person with whom you're working.

Otherwise, you're working in a vacuum. You have no meaningful information. Your plan probably won't match what the person does. Without participation from the other side, you've really got nothing—no matter how well you think the meeting went, and no matter what nice things the other person has to say about your products or services. Without a Next Step, you're selling in the dark and closing by chance.

And that, by the way, is what usually happens. People we talk to say nice things because they don't want to hurt our feelings, even when they've really decided not to work with us. The only mistake we can make in this situation is continuing to pour our time and energy into the relationship.

What matters is not what the person says, but what the person does to prove he or she is working through the sales process with us.

Most salespeople spend most of their time presenting to people who aren't really playing ball. Most salespeople simply guess about what should go into the plan they recommend. They have to guess because they've had no meaningful connection with the prospect and gathered no relevant information. They have no idea what the prospect is doing, so they have no idea what makes sense from the prospect's point of view. So they cover their eyes and pick a product or service from the brochure and pray that they've come up with something that matches the prospect's objectives. Sometimes what they suggest makes sense. Most of the time it doesn't.

Can you eventually sell something that way? Sure. Can you sell enough to hit your income goals? Maybe not.

Understand: The real tragedy isn't when the person says no to us. A clear, unambiguous no is actually great news! It means we don't have to spend any more time developing material for an inactive lead. The real tragedy comes when we give our presentation and the prospect says, "Hmmm . . . let me think about it. I'll call you sometime next week." Then we go back to the office and rework the proposal again and again and again with no commitment whatsoever from the other side.

If the person isn't responding to you at all or giving you any meaningful information, then there's really no ambiguity. There is no gray area. Someone who won't give you a clear Next Step is not consciously moving with you through the steps of the sales process—not pointing you toward the facts you have to learn—regardless of what he or she may say out loud about you and your company.

How do you get the person to give you meaningful information? To commit to a Next Step? By deliberately suggesting that Next Step in a way that's impossible to ignore and paying very, very close attention to what happens next. The people who then do respond to you are, by definition, your real prospects. They're the ones who are moving through the sales process with you. They're the ones you have to pay attention to.

If, on the other hand, the person you're talking to has demonstrated that he or she won't invest time in moving through the steps of the process with you, then guess what? You shouldn't invest any more of your own time in that relationship than absolutely necessary.

Again: There are four steps in the sales cycle. The last is what I'll call (for the sake of convenience) the close—the step where the person we're talking to decides that what we're recommending makes so much sense that he or she will commit to using it. The step before that is where we present the plan that makes sense. The step before that is where we gather information so that we know what makes sense. (That's the interviewing or information-gathering step; I consider it the make-or-break part of the relationship.) And the step before that is where we open up the relationship, or qualify the prospect.

Look again at the four steps. Notice that the information-gathering step is where we should spend most of our time; it's what enables us to make a recommendation that truly makes sense to the other person. (In fact, as you will learn in Chapter 25, the most effective closing strategy that you can use is simply an attempt to verify that what you have proposed really makes sense to the prospect: "It makes sense to me. What do you think?")

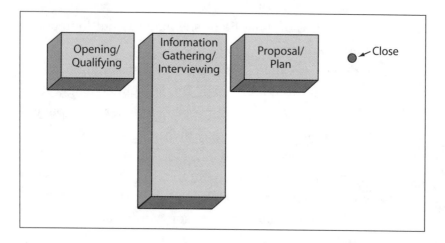

As I've pointed out a number of times, if we want the other person to use what we have to offer, the decision to work with us must make sense to that person. That seems obvious, but then so do a lot of things that salespeople ignore. At the risk of redundancy, let me repeat that whatever you eventually propose to the other person must be based on what makes sense to him or her.

That means that we have to learn—and confirm—what really makes sense to a prospect before we try to close. That means the plan we recommend should be one we develop side by side with the prospect. And here's the really amazing part: The prospect should know that we plan to ask for a commitment before we do so.

Your prospect should know that you plan to ask for the sale

before you ask for it.

You should see the looks I get from salespeople when I mention this point! But it's true. If we don't have clear participation from the prospect on one step, we can't move forward to the next one.

If we can't get explicit agreement from the prospect to move forward together in the first place, then we've really got nothing.

We must invest as much time as we possibly can in our prospects—the people who are actively playing ball with us. If our contact will not or cannot agree to a specific Next Step, and we develop a proposal anyway, we are wasting time. And that's something we can never get back.

That's why I advocate making noise during the selling process. Making noise yields responses; responses give you information.

Many people assume that when I say we should take a direct selling approach, we should make noise, we should do things that are impossible to ignore, we should cause appropriate tension at various points in the relationship, that I'm advocating a very pushy, low-information kind of sales process. Nothing could be further from the truth!

The approach I'm advocating is the best (and only) way to build your recommendation around what the other person is actually doing. We must instill a certain creative tension as we move forward from the first step to the second step, from the second step to the third step, and from the third step to the fourth step.

Why?

Because we can't assume that the prospect knows he or she is working with us unless we get clear evidence—based on action, not words—that this is the case. And building appropriate tension in the only relationship is the only way to get that evidence.

For instance, you should say, "Mr. Jones, you've given me a lot to think about at this meeting. I'd like to come back here next Monday at 10 AM and show you an outline of how we might be able to work together. Does that make sense?"

If the answer is yes, you've got a prospect. If the answer is no, you should find out why!

If, in the end, you don't get action-based evidence of involvement in the sale, you should find someone else to talk to!

FROM THE FRONT LINES

Shortly after I launched my sales training company, I was meeting with a prospect at a very large company in New York City. I had called on the phone and established a date and time for a face-to-face interview, and I was hoping to begin to gather information about this company so that I could put together the right sales training plan.

Calling to ask for an appointment in the first place was, of course, one way of throwing out the ball. But before I left the face-to-face meeting, I threw out the ball again.

At the end of half an hour, I looked at the president and said, "You've given me a lot to think about; what I'd like to do is come back here next Tuesday at 2 PM and show you some ideas about how we might be able to work together." Notice that by requesting a specific commitment from this contact, I was doing something impossible to ignore, something that required a response.

"Steve," the president said, "we don't work that way. Here's the way we work: You send us a proposal and we look it over. If we're interested, we'll give you a call. We don't schedule follow-up meetings with our training vendors. Pop your ideas into the mail and we'll call you if we're interested."

Here he was, telling me to take what I had learned, crunch it all into a document, and mail it to him without any further input, feedback, or commitment. I had thrown him the ball and he let it drop at his feet.

So what did I know at that point?

I knew that unless something changed in a hurry, there was absolutely no commitment in this relationship. The president wasn't willing to work with me to confirm what I'd learned about what his company did.

I tried throwing the ball out again.

After about five minutes of hemming and hawing, we hadn't made any progress whatsoever. The CEO insisted that there would be, could be, no follow-up meeting. I insisted that a follow-up meeting was essential if our two companies were to build a meaningful business relationship.

"Steve," he kept saying, "we don't work that way."

We had reached an impasse. And I had reached a critical moment in my career.

I looked the president straight in the eye and said, "Then I'm sorry, but I have to tell you that I don't work this way. I'm withdrawing from this project and I will not be submitting a bid. Thanks for your time."

I shook his hand and left the office. He was stunned.

When I tell that story to salespeople, they often look at me as though I were mad. With a potentially huge account, how could I possibly expect to change the rules of the game? And yet I believe that that experience was one of the most important and positive of my career. I think the company I built would have been far less successful if I'd failed to establish this principle in my own career and in our training materials. If I hadn't made my stand that day, I know for a fact that you would not be holding this book in your hands. On that day, I established a vitally important operating principle, one that would guide my business from that day forward. Here it is:

> People who don't make a commitment to me don't get
> my time.

People who don't make a commitment to you shouldn't get your time.

By withdrawing my time, effort, and attention from that project, I was maintaining a critical standard. If I could not continue to throw the ball to a qualified decision maker throughout the sales process who would throw the ball back to me, I simply would not take part in the sale. Period.

In that moment, I made a commitment to place the emphasis in my own selling routine exactly where it belonged: on face-to-face contacts with people who were demonstrably willing to commit their time, effort, energy, and attention—just as I was—to building a successful business relationship.

The truth is that salespeople all too often engage people in conversations that require no input, no responsibility, and no real intelligent discussion with anyone. By setting my standards a little higher, and knowing when I did not have someone to play ball with me, I was able to make a commitment to myself. I would spend all of my time working with people who were helping me to develop a plan that worked for them!

This was the turning point in my business and my career. After that meeting, I was able to spend all of my time working with people who actually did want to see, critique, revise, and customize my proposal! I was able to spend all of my time with people who really did want to play ball with me!

Simply by saying, "You've given me a lot to think about. I'd like to come back here next Tuesday at 2:00 to show you what I've come up with," I was increasing the tension in the relationship. I could tell exactly where I stood.

You can see now, I hope, that the kind of tension I'm talking about isn't a neurosis or a power trip; it's an intelligent, strategically designed information-gathering technique.

By throwing out the ball, you can find out precisely who is and who is not playing ball with you at any given moment. This book is about learning how to play ball in just the same way. It's about specific strategies you can use to do something appropriate that people cannot ignore, and must respond to somehow.

POINTS TO PONDER

- You probably already know, on an intuitive level, who's playing ball with you and who isn't.

- Focus your efforts on people who are willing to commit to a specific Next Step with you.

- The definition of selling is asking people what they do, how they do it, where they do it, when they do it, with whom they do it, and why they do it that way. Then, and only then, do we ask how we can help them do it better.

CHAPTER 4

...in which we discover the importance of getting on the other person's radar screen

"Get on the person's calendar—and find a way to stay there."

—*STEPHAN SCHIFFMAN*

*H*ave you won a spot on your prospect's schedule for a Next Step that will take place within the next two weeks?

If you haven't, there's a problem. You may be currently scheduled for a Next Step that is conveniently placed well beyond your prospect's radar screen. Next Steps that land outside the other person's radar screen don't count.

To illustrate this point, I'd like you to try this simple exercise. Take a moment to find a sheet of paper and a pen or pencil. On that sheet of paper, I want you to make a list of all the things that you want to do or are committed to do—tomorrow. Go from memory only. Don't leave anything out.

This portion of the exercise should take you at least five minutes. Please do not turn the page or continue reading in this book until you have made a detailed list of everything you are either already committed to do tomorrow or would like to accomplish on that day. (There's no need to complete the list in chronological order.)

Note: If tomorrow is Saturday or Sunday, please complete the exercise with Monday in mind.

Ready? Go!

By now, you should have a fairly lengthy list of things that are definitely on your to-do list for tomorrow. The list might include items such as:

- Review press release before it goes out—it's supposed to drop tomorrow afternoon!

- Set up conference call with English office; remember time difference

- Attend staff meeting (8:30–11:00)

- Review PowerPoint presentation on new training program

- Drive son to gymnastics class at 5:30

- Discuss new marketing plan

- Develop draft of new proposal

- Stop by mother-in-law's apartment after work (she's recovering from surgery)

- Change scheduled meeting with financial planner

- Call business contact my boss suggested I get in touch with

- Check in with contractor to discuss remodeling plan

- Revise project list

- Send e-mail to former colleague about upcoming party he's invited to

Once you've completed this exercise, please turn the sheet over and spend the same amount of time formulating a list of things you plan to be doing two weeks from now. Again: Don't check your calendar. Go from memory only. Don't worry about getting things down in the right order.

Only include specific, individual items that you know you plan to undertake on that day.

Ready? Go!

Something very interesting happens when we perform this exercise as part of our training programs. Not infrequently, the mental two-weeks-from-now to-do list is completely blank. Was yours?

Whether it was or not, let me go out on a limb here and make a prediction. If you're like the average overbooked professional, the first list is probably a good deal longer, and definitely a good deal clearer, than the second list.

It's just easier to visualize initiatives in the short term. What does that mean? It means, as a practical matter, that we give higher priority to things that are scheduled within the next two weeks.

So here's my question. If you're gauging commitment from someone with whom you want to work, on which side of the person's schedule would you rather be? The two-weeks-or-less side or the beyond-two-weeks side?

I hope that question answers itself. Just in case, though, let me share this reliable sales principle with you: At a point beginning two weeks from today, people stop paying close attention to what they've committed to. I've seen this demonstrated time and time again, and if you're honest with yourself, you'll realize that you have, too.

As a general but very reliable rule, people don't really take seriously any Next Steps that are placed more than two weeks in the future.

Time commitments that go beyond two weeks don't carry what advertising folks call "top-of-mind awareness." That's a fancy way of saying that, unless the future time commitment is something the person already has a strong emotional association to (such as a birthday or the April 15 tax filing deadline), it simply doesn't register as a priority.

In fact, I'll let you in on a little secret about the two-weeks-or-earlier principle. When people want to say no to us, but don't want to hurt our feelings, they do something very cagey. Can you guess what it is?

You've got it. They schedule us for a time beyond the radar screen, suspecting all the while that there's a pretty good chance they'll have to reschedule when something "more important" comes along.

And isn't that what often happens to these kinds of commitments? You get a voice mail from the person that says, "I just checked my calendar. I totally forgot we had that meeting tomorrow. I'm double-booked. Please forgive me. Call me when you can." If our meeting was really a top priority, what would that message sound like instead? "Gosh, I'm sorry. I double-booked myself. Can we meet the day after tomorrow at 10:00 AM instead?"

You may think I'm being cynical about human nature here, but these are simply business realities. People schedule us for a date outside of the radar screen so they won't have to give up the time that's important. In other words, they don't want to give up the part of their schedule that they're really using right now. When it dawns on them that the commitment has actually slipped into this two-week cycle, they usually try to reschedule or ignore us entirely for one of two reasons: (1) it is what they always meant to do, or (2) they simply wanted to postpone the whole question of whether or not they really wanted to meet with us.

To get an idea of what I'm talking about, take a look at this (common) sales exchange:

> *Salesperson:* "Mr. Prospect, I've learned a lot from our meeting, and here's what I'd like to do. Why don't I come back here next Monday at 10:00 and show you what we've come up with?"
>
> *Prospect:* "No, I need time to think about all this. Why don't you just call me sometime next month? Maybe we can set something up then."
>
> *Salesperson:* "Okay. I understand. How about the 14th of April at 3:00?"
>
> *Prospect:* "Sure."

Are you ready for the translation? Here's what's really being said:

> *Salesperson:* "Is this a big enough priority for you to meet again with me?"
>
> *Prospect:* "Gee, no, not really. I'll tell you what, though. I could make a feeble social gesture, just so I can be relatively sure that you won't go out and slash your wrists in the reception area on your way out of the office. Why don't you just call me—heh-heh— sometime next month?"

> *Salesperson:* "Thank God you didn't actually say the word no. Let's see, I'm supposed to get a specific date and time, I remember reading about that somewhere. How about the 14th of April at 3:00?"
>
> *Prospect:* "Whatever."

Now, if I were in this situation, I might try to salvage it by asking a "Gee, I didn't anticipate that" question.

As you'll see from the following dialogue, the "Gee, I didn't anticipate that" question can be one of your greatest sales resources. This kind of question works at virtually any point in the sales process. Note that it leads directly to a question to which the prospect must respond somehow.

> *Salesperson:* "Mr. Prospect, I've learned a lot from our meeting, and here's what I'd like to do. Why don't I come back here next Monday at 10:00 and show you what we've come up with?"
>
> *Prospect:* "No, I need time to think about all this. Why don't you just call me sometime next month. Maybe we can set something up then."
>
> *Salesperson:* "You know what? I really didn't anticipate that you'd say that. Usually, when a meeting goes as well as this one seemed to go, people are really eager to find a way to move forward. I'm just curious, why wouldn't you want to get together again and look at how we might be able to work together?"

(There follows a pause, perhaps even a fairly lengthy one. The skillful salesperson knows better than to speak at this point.)

> *Prospect:* "Well, you see, the thing is. . . ."

When the prospect includes the words "You see, the thing is" in any sentence, you win. Why? Because you get more information than you had before. You understand what's really happening. And if what follows is, "You see, the thing is, my budget is frozen for the next two years," you don't fall into the trap of spending hours and hours working on a proposal for this person "because you've got a follow-up appointment."

If the only date the person will give you is at a time more than two weeks from now, then the odds are that you don't really have a follow-up appointment.

The point is that people can say no to us without using the word no. And this is extremely likely to happen if we haven't yet established a good relationship with the person. Sometimes people disguise the no in nonbusiness settings, also. They may want to avoid hurting the other person's feelings, or they may not want to deal with a long, drawn-out discussion about why the relationship will not be moving forward. Regardless, it's in our best interests to understand that if there is no Next Step, we have, as a practical matter, been told no.

The past history of the relationship counts for a great deal, of course. Think of this situation: A single gentleman asks a single woman out on a date. Instead of saying yes, which is what the gentleman wants to hear, she tells him that she's having her hair done that night and she won't be able to make it.

Odds are, that's a no. But now picture a husband asking his wife whether she wants to go to the theatre on a certain evening. She says, "No, that's not going to work. I'm going to have my hair done that evening."

In the first-date situation, the "hair response" is almost certainly a disguised no answer, and should be regarded as such. But in the other situation—where a relationship already exists and is functioning on many levels—virtually the same response does not indicate a disguised no.

Just remember: Many positive-sounding responses that don't involve a Next Step actually reflect situations where the person has told us no. Such contacts must be put aside, at least for now.

FROM THE FRONT LINES

Not long ago, we trained a major advertising organization in our selling techniques. One of the strategies we passed along was designed to help people reestablish contact with customers who had received less than the company's best in the past.

You know the kind of customer I'm talking about: the one who received a shipment of inferior goods, or fell further down on the priority list than he or she should have, or didn't get a phone call returned quickly. The kind of customer who, for whatever reason, is likely to respond to any telephone call from you with stony silence. (Or worse: "Thanks for calling, Dave, but I checked with everyone on the team about the possibility of working with you and, unfortunately, we now hate you.")

As I say, we have developed a strategy for securing meetings with such accounts. It's among the most difficult things to do in the world of sales, and I would be lying to you if I told you that our strategy secured the meeting every single time. (Nothing secures any meeting in any situation every single time.) I will, however, suggest that the strategy I'm about to share with you, and that we shared with this particular advertising firm, is the most effective strategy for turning around relationships with angry customers.

What we told this advertising company to say was this: "You know, a lot of our customers, a lot of the people who are working with us now, once told me that exact same thing because of a bad experience they had with one of our previous account executives. What I'm trying to do now is set up a time so that you and I can discuss what we did for those customers, and why they're so happy with us now. Can we get together Thursday at 4:00?"

Notice again that this request features a specific suggested date and time for our next meeting. By specifying a date and time—one single date and one time of day—we are more likely to help turn the conversation away from extraneous issues (like what a company's formal procedures are or whether this client had a horrible response with his last advertising campaign) and more likely to focus the conversation on the topic we want to discuss—namely, the meeting.

At any rate, the strategy you just read is the one that we shared with this advertising organization. Not long after the training, we received a letter from one of the trainees informing us that the strategy had worked exactly as we had predicted it would. The dialogue went something like this:

> *Former Client:* "I told you I wasn't interested in wasting any more money with you guys."
>
> *Sales Rep:* "I certainly understand that and to tell you the truth, that's the reason I'm calling you in the first place. I've been thinking about some of our other current advertisers who once told me exactly what you're telling me, because they had had a problem with the previous account executive. What I'm asking for today is a slot on your schedule so you and I can discuss what we did for those clients and why they're so happy with us now. Can we get together Thursday at 4:00?"
>
> *Former Client:* "I'm really busy. Call me next quarter."

Now, the call could have stopped there. The rep could have given up or, even worse, dutifully scheduled a "meeting" for 90 days in the future. But that's not what happened. This sales rep knew the importance of throwing out the ball, of taking unignorable action to try to get on the prospect's radar screen.

Here's how the rest of the call went:

> *Sales Rep:* "I know you're busy, and I'm hoping I can have the opportunity to make you even busier. That's why all I'm asking for is an appointment for Thursday at 4:00." (There follows a pause, perhaps even a fairly lengthy one. The skillful salesperson knows better than to speak at this point.)
>
> *Former Client:*"Oh, all right. Come on in. I'll give you five minutes."
>
> *Sales Rep:* "Thanks. I'll see you then."

During the time between when the sales rep made that call and the date the meeting was scheduled, the sales rep did some research. Because he had the file showing what this advertiser had done previously and who his target customers were, he spent some time narrowing down the top four advertising applications that seemed to best meet the client's requirements. He then put together a sample schedule for those options that would target the audience the advertiser was after and deliver the appropriate frequency.

In other words, he worked his tail off to prepare for the meeting. He spent some time developing an answer to the former customer's question, "Why should I trust you again?" The time and effort he put in was completely justified because the meeting was actually on the prospect's radar screen.

The sales rep then created a one-page sheet that showed how the schedule he was suggesting would target prospects more effectively than the one that had been recommended previously. He went in the meeting with his single sheet of information poised to answer the former client's question.

The meeting started half an hour late; the former client made the sales rep wait in the lobby. Finally, the former client motioned for the sales rep to come in.

Twenty minutes later, the relationship had completely changed. The once-angry client was so impressed with the specific analyses and personal attention that the sales rep had assembled that he said the following: "This is all I really wanted. I wanted someone to do something for me that made sense. This is more than fair." At that point, he grabbed the proposal sheet from the sales rep's hand, signed it, and said, "I'm signing this before you change your mind." As the rep walked back out the door with a smile on his face and a signed agreement for a 52-week, $20,000 contract in hand, he reminded himself of the importance of asking clearly for commitments that are on the prospect's radar screen.

POINTS TO PONDER

- Ask directly and in an impossible-to-ignore way for a commitment within the next two weeks.

- If the commitment is not forthcoming, ask for it again, or ask a question that's preceded by some variation of the phrase, "I didn't anticipate that you'd say that."

- If you can't get some kind of clear time commitment for a discussion or meeting within the next two weeks, don't invest a great deal of time on that opportunity.

CHAPTER 5

...in which we learn to aim high

"He who would leap high must take a long run."

—DANISH PROVERB

*W*hen we train salespeople to set first appointments for meetings with prospects, we encourage them to call a person as high in the organization as they can, with one qualification. The person they call must be able to benefit directly from what they have to offer.

That means that if I'm selling copier toner, I'm probably not going to target the CEO of a Fortune 500 company to talk about that product, because he or she benefits only in an indirect way from what I sell. On the other hand, if I'm targeting a small family-operated business, it's quite possible that the company's owner would be a good person to talk to about copier toner. Why? Because in a business like that, the head person might well have to replace the copier toner now and then, and might even make a personal crusade out of choosing the right vendor for office products. Better prices or higher quality for copier toner could be a definite benefit in that business owner's life.

One half of the prospecting equation is calling people who can benefit directly from what we have to offer. The other half is aiming high.

Even if it's scary, aim high. Even if you've never talked to the head of a company before, aim high. Even if you've never asked a senior vice president for a face-to-face meeting before, aim high. Here's why: You get further by throwing out the ball to highly placed people than you do by throwing out the ball to people at the bottom of the organizational chart.

This is an extraordinarily important principle. It's one that can literally transform your career. Please take a moment now to think about how it applies to your daily prospecting work.

People at the very top of the organizational chart, as a general rule, make their living by taking action. People at the middle and bottom of the organization, as a general rule, make their living by taking orders. Whom would you rather talk to?

We've already learned that sales is a matter of challenging the status quo—of doing something impossible to ignore, and then following up with the people who respond positively to us. It follows, then, that if we choose people who spend most of their day taking action, we'll be more likely to get a response back. If, on the other hand, we target groups whose main purpose in life is maintaining the status quo, the results we get will be correspondingly weaker.

Ask yourself these questions: Who am I usually targeting in the prospect's organization? Why am I calling at that level? Does the person who holds this job make a living by taking action or by taking orders? Is there anyone else higher up in the organization I could target who could benefit directly from what my company has to offer?

Remember: We are trying to connect with people who will decide to use what we have to offer—forever. That means we want to avoid calling people who are unable to make that decision.

Remember: Close = Use.

Lots of salespeople tell me, "I've got a good routine here. I'm comfortable talking to low-level people. I learn a lot." The point of a prospecting call is to set an appointment. Period. Don't let force of habit dictate your income. Aim high. Change what you're doing. The rewards will make it easy for you to get comfortable with that routine, too.

In the end, it's a question of time. For a salesperson, time is the ultimate resource, and it's always in short supply. We want to throw out the ball to as many people as we possibly can who could actually decide to use us. If we spend all our time throwing out the ball to people who lack the authority to decide to work with us, we're going to waste too much of our (irreplaceable) time.

FROM THE FRONT LINES

One of our top salespeople routinely posts amazing prospecting ratios. His name is Gino Sette. Gino's calling strategies are worth reviewing closely. I often ask salespeople in my organization to model his calling approach.

First, a little background. In most cases, we are quite happy when a salesperson makes a daily commitment to making 15 dials, reaching seven decision makers, and scheduling one appointment. That is just a general yardstick for daily activity that tends to help people deliver on their income targets in our company. I don't know what your income targets are; those numbers might or might not make sense for you. That's really not important.

What is important is that our salespeople know that they need to schedule one appointment with a new decision maker each and every day to meet their long- and short-term goals. That is why they try to make, typically, the 15 calls every day in order to talk to those seven decision makers and set that one appointment.

Gino, however, did something very smart. He did not use those goals or those targets for daily appointments. He set a higher goal and came up with his own daily targets. He wanted two appointments a day to make his own closing numbers work. In other words, he held himself to a higher standard and decided that he had to generate two brand-new appointments with high-level decision makers, each and every day.

The reason I'm sharing Gino's story with you, though, is so I can show you how he made the two appointments a day happen. Instead of 15 calls, seven discussions with decision makers, and one appointment, Gino often posts daily numbers like this: 8 calls, 6 discussions with decision makers, and 2 appointments.

Those are absolutely mind-boggling ratios! When I share them with sales managers, they sometimes look at me as though I've gone mad. They seem to be thinking, no one posts daily numbers of eight, six, and two. It's not possible.

Gino has done it, though. What possible strategy could he have used to deliver such fantastic performance levels? Here are two of his secrets.

The first secret is that Gino makes a point of calling as many presidents and owners of organizations as he possibly can. Presidents and owners of organizations can benefit directly from sales training, which is what we sell. That's why Gino wants to reach them—not mid-level or low-level contacts—over the phone.

In the quite common event that the president, let's call him Mr. Big Shot, refers him to someone else in the target organization, Gino calls the person in question as soon as he knows that contact is likely to be at his or her desk. Gino begins his conversation with the new contact with the following sentence: "Did Mr. Big Shot tell you that I'd be calling?"

Think about the effect that a sentence like that has on the rest of the call.

"Hi Jack. This is Gino from D.E.I. Management Group. Did Mr. Big Shot tell you I'd be calling?"

That opening has proved highly effective in getting the new contact to open up, listen to what Gino has to say, and, eventually, schedule a face-to-face appointment. That's the real reason Gino's calling; he wants to know if he can meet face to face with you next Monday at 10:00.

Notice again that we do something deliberate and impossible to ignore—something that all but forces the other person to respond to us—in order for forward movement in the relationship to happen. The people who then do respond to us are, by definition, our prospects. Once they agree to meet with us, we know they're the people we want to pay attention to.

Look at how it works once more:

> *Prospect:* "Hi, this is Jack."
>
> *Gino:* "Hi, Jack, this is Gino from D.E.I. Management Group. Did Mr. Big Shot tell you I'd be calling?"
>
> *Prospect:* "Uh, I don't think so. What's up?"
>
> *Gino:* "Well, we're a sales training company. Earlier this morning, Mr. Big Shot and I were talking about a program that my company put together for the ABC Company that increased their total sales by 34 percent in just three months. He suggested you and I talk about it; I'd love to come by and show you what

we did for ABC. Could we meet this coming Tuesday at 10:00 in the morning?"

Prospect: "Tuesday at 10:00—let me see. No, Tuesday's no good. Could we shoot for Wednesday morning?"

Are you beginning to see how Gino posted those extraordinary numbers of his? If you still feel intimidated at the prospect of calling high in the organization, then I urge you to rethink your preconceptions and evaluate what they're costing you.

I promised you two strategies. The second strategy Gino uses, and one that we have trained for years as part of our appointment-making workshop, is always leave a voice mail message. Anytime he attempts to reach a given contact and that contact is away from his or her desk, Gino leaves a personalized voice mail message.

We train many salespeople who tell us that they don't believe in voice mail, which in the twenty-first century is a little bit like saying you don't believe in oxygen. It's pretty straightforward, as far as I can tell: If you sell for a living, you must prospect on a regular basis. If you prospect on a regular basis by phone, you must leave effective voice mail messages.

Gino, like the rest of our staff, uses a message outline that he adapts by industry. He takes a good look at our list of current and past customers. He then memorizes one company for each major industry that he was targeting. When it comes time to leave a voice mail message for someone who worked in the energy industry, his voice mail message sounds like this:

"Hi, Mr. Prospect, this is Gino Sette from D.E.I. Management Group. I'm calling regarding Huge Energy Corporation. Please give me a call at 212-555-5555. Once again, that's 212-555-5555."

Huge Energy Corporation, of course, is one of our customers. When the contact calls back, Gino will instantly reference the work we've done with Huge Energy as the reason for his call; he wants to talk about that program with the prospect.

That's a pretty simple message, but look at it closely and you will see why it works so well. First and foremost, it references the prospect's name. That's important, because people tend to pay more attention to messages that reference their name first. Second, the message introduces the caller by name and company, but not by job title. That is important because many decision makers instantly screen out or delete messages that they know to be left by salespeople. Third, the message quickly offers an answer to the looming question that is on everyone's mind when it comes time to review voice mail messages: What's this all about? This particular message is "about" a company in this prospect's very own industry—a competitor or, at the very least, a company of which the person has heard.

That message is short, direct, and impossible to ignore. It's a message that throws out the ball and encourages people to throw the ball back. The people who do respond to that message are the people on which we're going to focus.

Did you notice that the message includes Gino's telephone number twice? All too often when people leave voice mail messages, they speak incredibly fast and reference their phone number only once. The person moving through the list of messages can't keep up!

Gino, like the other salespeople we've trained, gets remarkable results with that kind of message. You can too, if you keep the message short and focused, follow the outline I've described here, and remember to point it at the highest-ranking person who could benefit from what your company offers.

You should also make a point of monitoring your own activity. If you do, you'll be able to set your own priorities and establish your own goals. Work backwards and figure out how many sales you need to close this quarter. Then look at your own calling numbers and selling activity. Monitor what you do for two to three days, or perhaps a week. Look at your numbers closely and ask yourself: How many dials did it take me to generate a conversation with a decision maker? How many conversations with decision makers does it take me to generate a single appointment? How many visits (first appointments plus follow-up appointments) does it take me to deliver a single sale? How many sales do I need to get my quota this year? What has happened recently in the economy, and how do those changes affect the activity I must post each day in order to hit my target for first appointments?

> *Set goals based on your own activity, and monitor your own ratios closely.*

If you work through all of those questions in detail, and monitor your numbers over time, you will have a clear idea of exactly how many dials you need to make each and every day to support your income goals. As you monitor your ratios and as you get better at making calls, you will see something interesting start to happen. The higher up in the target organization you call and the more direct you are about what you think should happen next, the better your numbers will look.

POINTS TO PONDER

- Call high.

- Always leave a message.

- Set your own goals and monitor your own calling ratios.

CHAPTER 6

... in which we learn the benefits of calling off-peak

"Nothing is graceful that we have not made utterly our own."

—*JEREMY COLLIER*

Call off-peak. Live off-peak! You'll connect with more people.

If you're having trouble getting in touch with decision makers, it may be because you are calling at the wrong times. Calling restaurant owners around noon, for instance, may not be the best idea, because these people often have to contend with a lunch rush that leaves them preoccupied, to say the least.

Guess what? Sales is not your typical nine-to-five job. As a general rule, you should schedule your prospect calling time for very early or very late in the day. If you do this, you'll probably find the people you do reach more receptive to the Next Step you're proposing. Remember: You're not calling for your health. You're calling to introduce your company briefly and propose a specific, impossible-to-ignore course of action. If the person reacts positively to your suggestion, you'll know that you've established forward motion in the relationship.

Sales is not your typical nine-to-five job.

Calling at a time when the person isn't likely to be immersed in the demands of the day is a great way to make it more likely that you'll win some kind of forward motion, and also a great way to get around any gatekeepers that may be standing in your way.

FROM THE FRONT LINES

Not long ago, I got a call from my publisher telling me that a major Midwestern company had ordered 400 copies of one of my books. Sensing that this lead could turn into a good prospect for face-to-face training from our company, I tried to call the person who had ordered the books. The person's administrative assistant, however, informed me that her boss was busy all day, all week, all month. She'd let him know that I called. If he was interested, he'd give me a call back.

That's called end of forward motion in the relationship! What would you have done to make something happen in such a situation?

Here's what I did: I waited until after 6 PM Chicago time that night, used the phone system to figure out the person's direct extension, made a note of the number, and then called directly. Guess who was sitting at his desk? The contact and I had a great call. I scheduled the appointment, and eventually closed the sale!

POINTS TO PONDER

- Accept that sales is not a nine-to-five job.

- Call off-peak.

- When you reach people before or after hours, you're more likely to establish forward motion in the relationship.

CHAPTER 7

... in which we learn the importance of being specific about what we want first from the prospect

"The secret of success is constancy to purpose."

—BENJAMIN DISRAELI

I've been training people to make cold calls for nearly 30 years. This book isn't really meant to focus closely on showing you how to do that (although I have included a brief overview of the topic in Appendix A, Seventeen Keys to Getting More Appointments). I do want to focus here, though, on an important principle that supports the cold calling process as a whole.

The point of the prospecting call is not to sell something to the person who answers the phone. Rather, the point of the prospecting call is to get the person's initial negative responses out on the table so you can turn that initial negative response around and focus on asking directly for a face-to-face appointment by specifying a specific date and time to get together.

*Use the prospecting call to get negative responses out of
the way, turn them around, and request the appointment
by proposing a single specific date and time.*

By approaching the cold call in this way, you will be doing something deliberate and impossible to ignore. You will basically be controlling the flow of the conversation, so that you get some kind of response from the other person. The people who do respond positively to you will, by definition, be prospects; they're the ones on which you should focus your attention.

FROM THE FRONT LINES

Some years back, we trained a remarkable young lady in Canada in our Appointment Making workshop. That program is, I think, the essential first step to taking control over your income as a salesperson. It contains a lot of information. This woman, however, only got one memorable element from that program. But she made it the right one!

This young woman completed before and after tapes of live calls. The tapes illustrated exactly what she had picked up and showed how dramatically her calling style had changed as a result of taking our program.

The before calls were hesitant, meandering, inappropriately phrased, and often hard to understand. There was a brief introduction, a sentence or two about what her company did, and then a mumbled request for a meeting. The after calls, on the other hand, were poised, confident, easy to understand, and focused almost obsessively on a single sentence: "Can we get together next Tuesday at 2:00?"

Here's the point: Her career has taken off like a rocket ship since she took that program. Our training, more or less, transformed her career and rocketed her to top salesperson status within her organization. She was able to secure enough first appointments with enough new prospects to maintain her income goals, and she did so by turning around objections simply by saying, "I understand what you mean. Let's get together and talk about it. How's this Tuesday at 2:00?"

Let me repeat. She basically got only one idea from the whole day's training: When in doubt, ask for the appointment by specifying a single date and time! And it changed her career.

Clearly, she picked the right principle to build a cold calling campaign around. If you can make the calls and set the appointments, you can set and maintain the right minimum level of first appointments for your income goals. If you can do that, you'll be fine. (At D.E.I., each of our sales reps maintains a constant level of at least 15 new first appointments. If the level of new contacts drops below that level, we know we're going to have problems hitting our target numbers.)

Suppose someone tells me to call back in a month. That's not a Next Step. That's an opportunity for a follow-up call. Here's what it might sound like.

> "Mr. Rodriguez, back on January 3rd, you suggested that I get in touch with you around this time to set up a meeting. Could we meet this coming Wednesday, March 16th, at 2:00 PM.?"

What kind of a response am I going to get from a call like that? Well, a good percentage of the time, I'll find myself on the receiving end of a question like, "What did you say you do again?" At that point I can offer a brief summary, and I do mean brief, of what D.E.I. does, and after a sentence or two, I can ask a question that bounces the ball back into the prospect's court once again.

For instance, "Just out of curiosity, have you worked with an outside sales trainer before?" Note that this question focuses on what I have to offer a prospective customer, and focuses directly on a response that I feel comfortable handling.

When the contact comes back to me and says, "Yes, we have done sales training in the past." I can say, "Oh really? Whom have you worked with?" That will get me a company name, at which point I can say, "Well, that's really why we ought to get together, because we've worked with a lot of companies who once worked with ABC Company. Why don't we meet Wednesday at 2:00?"

If, on the other hand, the person says, "Gee, we've never worked with a sales training company before." I can turn that response around just as easily. Can you guess what I'm going to focus on? You've got it—the possibility of a meeting on Wednesday at 2:00 PM. What I'd say would sound like this:

> "That's really why we *ought* to get together, because we've worked with a lot of companies in the widget industry who handled all their training internally until they saw how we could help improve their bottom line. I'd love to get together with you to show you what we've done in your industry. How's Wednesday at 2:00 PM?"

Throw out the ball. See what happens.

By this point, you should be fairly comfortable with the idea of refocusing your initial telephone contacts on the narrow subject of *scheduling a first appointment* with the prospect. Once you have set the appointment, thank the person for his or her time, politely disengage from the conversation, and end the call.

It's extremely important not to allow an appointment-setting call to degenerate into an attempted sale over the phone.

Remember our four steps of selling. We've asked for the chance to open up the relationship, and we've just received it. That's enough for now. In a face-to-face selling environment (which is my favorite selling environment), the first key to success lies in piling up enough first appointments to support your income goals. The best way to do that is to avoid long prospecting calls. Long drawn-out conversations with prospects have a way of eating up time, effort, and energy, and result in cancellations. (The standards are different, of course, if your job is to close sales over the phone. See Appendix B, Some Thoughts on Telesales.)

POINTS TO PONDER

- Focus your prospecting calls on a single, all-important issue—namely, whether or not the prospect will meet with you at a particular date and time.

- Be sure to read Appendix A, Seventeen Keys to Getting More Appointments. It will give you important information about reaching out to new people by phone.

- If you are selling over the phone rather than attempting to set face-to-face meetings with prospects, read Appendix B, Some Thoughts on Telesales.

CHAPTER 8

...in which we find out how to make forward progress even when the prospect says no

"When you encounter difficulties and contradictions, do not try to break them, but bend them with intelligence."

—SAINT FRANCIS DE SALES

*D*o you remember that powerful calling strategy of Gino's that I told you about—calling high in the organization and then following up with, "Did Mr. Big Shot tell you I'd be getting in touch with you?" Here's an equally effective way to turn a "cold call" into a "warm call."

Suppose you're making calls as a field salesperson. That usually means your goal is to meet with prospects in person. Think of the total number of calls you'll be making over the course of a week. Whatever that number is, let's call it X. Some of those calls are going to move forward to what I call a Next Step—probably a face-to-face appointment at the prospect's office, but definitely *some* kind of clear commitment of the prospect's time and attention at some point over the next two weeks.

*Your goal is always to throw out the ball and attempt to
get the other person's agreement to proceed with you to
some kind of Next Step.*

Some number of those calls, though, won't move forward
to a Next Step. We'll call that number Y.

Over the course of the week, then, you have the opportunity to ask Y number of people—directly, and in an impossible-
to-ignore way—for referrals. That will lead you to a total number of referrals that I'll call Z.

If you do this right, you'll be able to get in touch with Z
number of people by saying something like this: "Did Ms. Refer-
rer tell you I'd be getting in touch with you?"

FROM THE FRONT LINES

"Before our training with D.E.I., our telesales group
had a 10 percent closing ratio. Afterwards, the number
was 14.6 percent, and sales arising from referrals have
increased dramatically."

That's the feedback we received from a telesales manager at
one of the nation's largest telecommunications firms. The dramatic results his team posted took place as a result of a simple
and highly effective strategy for asking for referrals. One salesperson we trained in this method managed to set a new team
record for the total number of referral-driven sales.

Here's how we helped that team improve their numbers.
We told them to throw out the ball in a way that was impossible
to ignore. They were simply to introduce a basic question into

their calling routine. The question sounded like this: "Do you know of anybody else I should be talking to about this?"

It's startling in its simplicity, isn't it?

Most of the people we train are hesitant to ask a question like that. We get any number of objections about it. Isn't this question too pushy? Is it too direct? Does it destroy the possibility of a later relationship with this prospect? Is it likely to be perceived as a breach of etiquette?

The answer to all of these questions is no.

When you think about it, if the question is delivered in the right tone of voice, there is no way there can be any negative fallout from this query. Keep it light; keep it casual; keep it focused. Throw out the ball. Say, "Hey, do you know of anybody else I should be talking to about this?"

I recommend that if you're calling to set face-to-face appointments, you only ask this question of people who have declined your attempt to set a meeting. (Again, it's important to close out the conversation quickly and politely once you've set the time and date for your Next Step.) If, on the other hand, you're not setting appointments, but rather trying to close the sale over the phone, then I'd say you can give this strategy a try on just about every call. That's what the telecommunications salespeople I mentioned did!

By incorporating that simple but vitally important technique, that telesales team was able to exceed their quota by 10 percent and set a new record on a single day that more than doubled the daily quota!

Most of the advice that you'll read in this book is applicable to both in-person and telephone sales work. But this particular strategy seems to be most effective when used over the phone, either to attempt to set up a first appointment or as a result of a sales designed for a one-call or multiple-call close.

Don't simply assume that you can't come right out and ask directly for a referral. You can, and we've trained hundreds of sales teams to increase their sales totals in a measurable way by doing just that!

POINTS TO PONDER

- Ask for the referral in a direct, unambiguous way.

- Keep the tone light and open.

- Throw out the ball and see what happens!

CHAPTER 9

...in which we learn how to make something out of nothing

"To know oneself, one should assert oneself."

—ALBERT CAMUS

Believe it or not, contacts will agree to meet with you for "reasons" you propose that seem, from the standpoint of pure logic, not to exist. Some of my biggest customers started out as cold contacts that I appealed to with no referral, no track record in the industry, and no earthly reason for the call. The point is, I made a reason for the call. I made the act of producing creative tension on the phone—the act of asking specifically for a Next Step in a way that was difficult to ignore—the point of the call. As a result, I got the Next Step and, eventually, the sale.

FROM THE FRONT LINES

The minute one of our salespeople schedules an out-of-state appointment, that person will swing into a special, heightened level of phone activity, calling as many prospect companies residing in that same metropolitan area as possible. Our Vice President of National Sales, Lynne Einleger, is famous for calling up prospects and using an incredibly effective calling script. It sounds something like this:

> Hi, Mr. Jones, this is Lynne Einleger calling from D.E.I. Management Group. I'm not sure if you're familiar with us or not. We're a sales training company. We have worked with firms such as AT&T, Exxon, EMC, and Blue Cross/Blue Shield. The reason I'm calling you specifically today is that I just scheduled an appointment with Consolidated Widget Company in Philadelphia. I'm going to be in your neighborhood next week. I'd love to get together with you to talk about what we've been able to do for some of the companies in the _____ industry. How's Tuesday at 10:00?

Now, logically, how much sense does that make? "I'm going to be in Philadelphia. We should get together." If she lived and worked in Philadelphia, would she still be able to schedule an appointment by saying the same thing to the contact? Maybe not. But the notion of "I'm flying in to your city" seems to capture people's attention.

And the technique works. It works because it's compelling, it illustrates our success, and it asks for a Next Step in a direct way that's virtually impossible to ignore. We have secured a truly startling number of appointments in outlying cities simply by pointing out that we are going to be in the neighborhood anyway to visit with another company. When we suggest that we get together in order to take advantage of the fact that we are going to be in Philadelphia or Dallas or Boston or whatever, the prospect's response is usually quite positive. For some strange reason, the fact that you are willing to fill in a travel date meeting with another prospect inspires a certain kind of respect and gratitude.

I think a lot of the companies that Lynne calls using this script are simply impressed by our initiative and wish that their own salespeople would follow up with out of town prospects in much the same way!

By the way, there are lots of variations on this strategy. For instance: "Hi, I'm on the road next week; I'm going to be in Chicago. We should get together. How's Monday at 10:00?" Believe it or not, it works!

There are a number of other intriguing something-out-of-nothing calling variations. Here are a few of my favorites:

- *"I was just thinking of you."* This is a great strategy to use with people who have blown you off in the past, or with whom you have worked with in the past and want to re-establish contact. Believe it or not, you can lead the conversation with, "Hi John, I was just thinking about you. I thought we should try and get together next week to catch up. How's Tuesday at 2:00?" And a substantial percentage of the people you connect with will agree!

- *"I'm here in Philadelphia and I was thinking of you. Let's get together."* This variation shows the prospect that you are eager to connect while you are in his or her home town. It's better of course, to make the call a week or so ahead of time, but this approach can also deliver positive results.

- *"I'm on the road in Philadelphia. Why don't we get together?"* —when the person you're calling is in Dallas! Again, there seems to be no logical reason why the simple fact of being on the road should open a door for you in a town that is several states away, but the strategy does, in fact, work. We think the reason prospects respond to it is that this person is traveling a great deal and wants to make the prospect a part of his or her travel plans. It's flattering!

The point is, once you have used your standard script on a prospect, there is no reason not to call again.

Find a reason to throw out the ball and the odds are you'll find a way to make something out of nothing.

POINTS TO PONDER

- Call to set up a meeting because you've just scheduled a meeting in the prospect's town.

- Call to set up a meeting because you are on the road or plan to be on the road.

- Call to set up a meeting because you were just thinking about the prospect.

CHAPTER 10

...in which we learn the importance of getting a commitment before we leave the meeting

"What we seek, we shall find—what we flee from flees from us."

—RALPH WALDO EMERSON

*W*e have a policy at our organization never to leave the site of a prospect meeting without having asked for some type of commitment. Our motto is simple: Get them to do something—anything.

If the person won't agree to do something with us by the end of the first meeting, we do not consider the person a prospect. And that's an important issue, considering that everyone on staff has strict quotas for active prospects. As a practical matter, we usually want the first appointment to conclude with a *specific, impossible-to-ignore request for a second appointment at a particular date and time.*

My experience is that it is significantly easier to get a first appointment than it is to get a second appointment. It is for this reason, I think, that most salespeople avoid asking for the second appointment while they are on the site of their first appointment. They are afraid the prospect will shoot them down or reject them by rejecting their request to get together once again.

Here's my question for salespeople who wish avoid that kind of rejection: Would you rather be rejected a week, or a month, or a quarter later, and have that dead-end relationship eat up time and energy you spent preparing proposals? Or would you rather know about the rejection right away so you can focus your time and attention on another prospect?

Remember: We must do something deliberate and impossible to ignore—something that all but forces the other person to respond to us—in order for a sale to happen. The people who then do respond to us are, by definition, our prospects; they're the ones on which we should focus our attention. The people who don't respond to us are simply opportunities.

The people who don't respond to our efforts to win a Next Step are simply opportunities for future sales. They are not active prospects.

FROM THE FRONT LINES

Recently, I was meeting with a major prospect in the high-tech field. Our first meeting had gone very well. If I had been a disciple of the most common form of sales training and instruction, I might have concluded our meeting by saying something like this:

"You know, Ms. Jones, I think this meeting has gone really well and you've given me a great deal to think about. Would it be all right if I called you next week to set up another appointment so we can review how we might be able to work together?"

My goal in this book is to make you see that a question like that equals sales *death.* It equals death because it is basically asking the prospect for his or her permission *not* to get involved in the sale. A request like that is asking the prospect for consent for a Next Step on our part with no parallel buy-in or responsibility on the *prospect's* part!

People who teach negotiating seminars often say that the best way to negotiate is to grant a concession only after you have received a concession from the other side. Without becoming too adversarial about the selling process, I want to suggest to you that a very similar principle is at work in the fateful and all-important opening stages of any new business relationship. Ask yourself: *What are you getting in return from this person?*

Here is what I said to secure a Next Step with the decision maker at that high-tech firm. Notice how different it is from the "death rattle" wrap-up you read a moment ago.

> "You know, Ms. Jones, you've given me a lot to think about today. What I'd like to do is go back to my office, think about what we went over today, and come back next Tuesday at 2:00 with Steve Bookbinder, who is the person we would want to have conduct the training if you decided to go forward and work with us. At that point, Steve and I could show you some of our thinking about the ways we might be able to work together. How does that sound?"

The difference between the first end-of-meeting request ("May I call you at some unspecified point in time to set up the Next Step?") and the second ("Will you meet with key person X next Tuesday at 2:00 with me?") could not be clearer. Notice that the second way is an example of throwing out the ball. I've made a suggestion; the other person has to react. I am assuming that next Tuesday at 2:00 PM is a good time. The only real question is if my contact is willing to meet with Steve Bookbinder at that point.

By forcefully stating the specific Next Step I want to have from my contact, I was able to move the relationship forward, schedule a meeting within the all-important "next two weeks" time frame, and, eventually, close a huge sale for my organization. How much of my time would I have wasted if I had closed the meeting by doing what most salespeople do—merely asking permission to call at some open-ended date in the future?

Look at it again:

"You know what? We should really get my manager/ our technical person/our writer in here for you to talk to. Can we come by to talk to you next Tuesday at 2:00?"

Far from being a sign of weakness, bringing in your boss or another expert is actually a sign of strength, and an excellent way to move the relationship forward.

Choose your proposed Next Step carefully, and match it to what you've learned about the prospect.

Often, when we can't secure a Next Step, it's because we ask for one that's too difficult or not helpful enough to the contact. Make sure the Next Step you offer is incredibly easy and clearly helpful to the other person.

If you are having problems getting to the Next Step with a given prospect, it's probably because the Next Step you are asking for is not easy enough, or not seen as helpful by the prospect.

What matters when it comes to Next Steps is not what we suggest, but what the other person actually agrees to. Consider the following exchange:

> *You:* "I'd like you to come to our event next Tuesday at 2:00 so you can meet our president. How does that sound?"
>
> *Prospect:* "Gee, that sounds interesting. Give me your e-mail address and I'll let you know."

This is not a Next Step! Propose another one either now or by phone after the meeting. Make sure it's easy to agree to. Make sure it's helpful to the other person. Consider suggesting an on-site review or analysis by you or another team member. George Richardson, one of our top salespeople, makes a habit of proposing himself as the Next Step. He offers to interview salespeople, evaluate what they're doing, and present a report to his contact on what he's learned. It's an extremely effective approach.

One of our senior salespersons, Stacia Skinner, attributes her high commissions to a simple comment: "You know what? You really ought to meet my boss."

These salespeople use the manager as the reason for scheduling another meeting with prospects who represent the potential for serious income. They always have got a good excuse to ask the best new prospects for the all-important Next Step.

This is one of the most effective—and frequently overlooked—strategies for making something positive happen in the sales relationship. It's a great example of throwing out the ball in a way that is absolutely impossible to ignore, and adding value to the prospect's world.

So, what is your Next Step strategy? What's the primary Next Step you're after? What's your backup? Will you conclude the next meeting by asking for a

- meeting to review a preliminary proposal with the prospect?

- meeting to introduce the prospect to your boss (or a technical expert within your organization)?

- meeting to demonstrate your product or service?

- commitment from the prospect to visit your facility or attend one of your company's events?

POINTS TO PONDER

- Always ask for some form of Next Step at the conclusion of your meeting with the prospect.

- Usually, when we fail to get agreement to a Next Step, it's because we've asked for a step that is either too difficult for the other person to commit to at this stage of the relationship, or not helpful enough to the contact.

- Every prospect is different, so look closely at the Next Step you plan to ask for at the conclusion of your next meeting. Make sure the Next Step you propose is easy to commit to and helpful in a way that will be immediately obvious to your prospect. ("What if I talked to your employees, did a short summary of what other companies are doing with us in this area, and then came back here to review that with you? Would that make sense?")

- What really counts is not what next step we've asked for, but what the other person has specifically agreed to.

CHAPTER 11

…in which we learn to use questions to move the sales cycle forward

"If you would persuade, you must appeal to interest, rather than intellect."

—BENJAMIN FRANKLIN

*O*ur initial meetings with a prospect are critical information-gathering periods. The only way we can gather the right information is by asking the right questions.

We can't depend on the other person to volunteer the right information about what he or she does. We have to be willing to ask, in a way that's impossible to ignore, about what the individual and the organization is hoping to accomplish. There's a name for people who respond to our questions by giving us information that shows us what the individual and the company are trying to do. They're our prospects; they're the people on which we should be focusing our attention.

FROM THE FRONT LINES

Here are five questioning areas I hold my own salespeople accountable for at weekly sales meetings. If they can't come up with the right answers in each of these areas, I know they haven't done their job correctly during the information-gathering phase.

Question 1: *How Did This Person Get the Job?*

How did the prospect get his or her job?

If you're talking to the founder of the company, what's the story about how the company got started?

Put the focus on the other person, especially during the early meetings. Ask about his or her career path.

To find out how the person got the job, you can ask, "I'm just curious, how does someone become a vice president of widget operations/personnel director/whatever?" Write down the answers you get. If you don't know how the person got the job, you don't know enough!

Question 2: *What's the Contact's Role, and What's His or Her Current Plan?*

Is your contact a leader or a follower in the organization? Can the person you're talking to set the budget? The timetable? The agenda?

Has this person ever worked with a company like yours before? Ask!

Ask, "Did you get promoted into this position, or were you recruited from outside?" (The implication that your contact might have been recruited probably won't hurt your rapport with the contact.) Follow up with, "When did that happen?" You can also ask, "When did you become responsible for hiring/new product development/training/whatever?" *Write down the answers you get.* These answers will give you insight not only into how the person got this job, but whether or not he or she wanted it in the first place. Often, we connect with "decision makers" whose primary objective is to get someone else to take over responsibility in a certain area. If that's the case, you should know.

Ask about the kinds of projects the person has worked on recently. What role in shaping the agenda, the timetable, and the budget did your contact play? Again: Is this person a leader or a follower?

Is your contact the decision maker? The best way to find this out is to ask *indirectly.* Don't ask: "Are you the decision maker?" It's too early in the relationship to pose a question like that. Instead, ask:

- "How did you decide to do this in the past?"

- "Why did you do it that way?"

- "I'm just curious, what would you have done in this area if I hadn't gotten in touch with you?" (This is one of my favorites. It's absolutely essential—don't skip it!)

Explore the answers you receive. Has any action been taken up to this point? Who was involved? What were the criteria for (for instance) selecting vedors? What is the main goal of the initiative?

Ask, "Just out of curiosity, what were you planning to do in this area if I hadn't called you?"

The answers you get will tell you what you need to know about this person's status. Your prospect should be either the decision maker or a person who has influenced a comparable purchase decision in the past. You're looking for someone who can move the process forward for you.

When in doubt, ask, "How/why did you decide to do such-and-such?" If the person doesn't know, try to arrange a meeting with the person who does know. That's the leader who controls budgets, timetables, and agendas.

What is your prospect's current plan for dealing with the situation? What role will your prospect play in implementing that plan? *Write down the answers you get.*

Question 3: Why Isn't the Prospect Using You Now?

The next time you meet with a new prospect for the first time, consider asking this question after the initial meet-and-greet phase of the meeting:

> "I checked my records and saw that you're not currently a customer of ours. I was just curious, why not?"

Write down the answer you get. This simple query has produced astonishing results for the salespeople we have trained. In most cases, it instantly reveals the prospect's status quo and makes it obvious to other parties whether there is a basis for continuing the business relationship beyond the first meeting.

Isn't that what you really want to know?

Look at it again:

> "Mr. Smith, I took a look at our computer list before I came over here and I noticed that you're not on our list of customers. I'm just curious, why not?"

This question instantly clarifies the status quo and launches the information-gathering step. And yet virtually all the salespeople we train, at least at first, are hesitant about using it. Try this question before you dismiss it. It has delivered significant revenue for us and for the people we train. With this question, you instantly begin getting the information you want. You control the flow of the conversation, and you find out what obstacles, if any, are keeping you from working with this person.

Question 4: *What Are the Individual's Goals?*

What is the most important thing your prospect's trying to accomplish on an individual level?

Individual aspirations may differ sharply from goals that your prospect shares as part of the work group. For instance: If your prospect's personal goal is to get another job within 30 days, you should know about that, even though it may not be a goal he or she would discuss with the boss.

To find out about individual goals, ask, "Just out of curiosity, where do you see yourself going in this job? What's most important to you here?" Or, "Based on what you've told me, *X* seems to be a major priority for you personally. I'm just curious why?"

You can also ask, "I'm just curious, what do you do here?" *Write down the answer you get.*

Question 5: *What Are the Organizational Goals?*

What is the most important thing your prospect is trying to accomplish on an organizational level?

Here are questions you can ask to find that answer:

- "I'm curious, what are you trying to make happen here over the next 30 days?"

- "How does your company sell its product/service?"

- "How many people work here? Do they report to you?"

- "How many people do you work with who operate out of other locations?"

- "How is your organization structured? How many offices/locations do you have?"

- "What are you doing right now to handle challenge X?"

- "What made you decide to make X a priority right now?"

- "What made you decide to call us?"

- "What kinds of new customers are you trying to attract?"

- "Who do you consider to be your biggest competitor? Why?"

- "How do you distinguish yourself from the competition in an industry like this?"

- "How's business?"

- "Is your industry changing? How?"

- "What was the past quarter/year like for you?"

Write down the answers you get.

Hallmarks of Effective Interviewing

Effective interviewing takes time. Don't rush the discussion.

Effective interviewing is not product-focused or service-focused. Don't pull out your brochure and start reading it verbatim.

Effective interviewing doesn't immediately jump to the presentation. Make no recommendation before you are certain you know what the person is trying to get done.

Effective interviewing builds around the right questions. Focus on variations on the big issues: "What did you do in the past?" and "What are you trying to accomplish now?" Four steps that will allow you to lead, or take charge of, a sale are:

1. Ask what the person does, has done, and is planning to do.

2. Listen (and take careful notes).

3. Learn. . . .

4. Offer an *impossible-to-ignore* Next Step that will help the person attain his or her objective. Once you make a clear offer to help, monitor the reaction you get closely. If the person responds positively, you still have a prospect. If not, you have to strategize and propose another Next Step.

Four Levels

Inefficient salespeople head down lots of blind alleys because they don't ask prospects meaningful questions. Sometimes, they don't ask any questions at all.

Such salespeople use what we call "slapshot" selling. They try to close from the moment they walk in the door, and they respond to virtually everything the prospect says with some variation on, "Hey, we've got just what you need. We can do the same thing, only better."

How do you feel when someone—say, a telemarketer—uses this approach on you? Don't you think to yourself, "This person knows nothing about me. I can't take any of these promises seriously."?

There are four levels on the sales continuum. The higher we move with the customer on the sales continuum, the better our information gets and the more valuable the relationship becomes.

The first (and lowest) level is the *seller*. This level features virtually no trust or information. It's typically a one-time-sale mentality on both sides of the transaction.

The *vendor* relationship features a little trust and a little information. You're "in the Rolodex," and future business is a possibility, but not a sure thing.

The *supplier* relationship is higher still. It features significant levels of trust and information. There is predictable repeat business, and you help the customer develop criteria for doing business and resolving challenges.

At the highest level is the *partner* relationship. Here, there are extremely high levels of trust and information. You function as a strategic partner, and you and the customer are mutually dependent on each other for success.

The third level on the sales continuum—that of the supplier—is one most salespeople consider their ultimate goal with the prospect/customer. This is a mistake because it is not the highest level.

Partnership with our customers is the highest level on the continuum, and the ultimate goal of any sale we make.

Most salespeople do not explore their relationships with customers deeply enough to move forward to the partner level. As a result, they go back and forth between vendor and supplier with their "best" customers, never realizing that a whole new level of cooperation—and income!—is waiting at the next level.

POINTS TO PONDER

- Find out how the person got the job.

- Find out what the current plan is and what the contact's role in implementing that plan is.

- Find out why they aren't using you now.

- Find out the individual goals.

- Find out the organizational goals.

- Write your answers down.

- Know the hallmarks of effective interviewing.

- Don't be a slapshot salesperson.

CHAPTER 12

... in which we find out new ways to wake up sleeping prospects

"'Be bold! Be bold!' and everywhere— 'Be bold;
Be not too bold!' Yet better the excess
Than the defect; better the more than less."

—HENRY WADSWORTH LONGFELLOW

*I*n Chapter 9, you learned about the "I was just thinking of you" call, which is a great way to bring life back to a dormant relationship with a prospect. There are a number of others. All operate on the same principle: Find something appropriate to do that the other person *can't ignore*. Suggest some kind of Next Step as a result. Follow up appropriately if the person responds.

> *Don't pester people. Find a reason to call that adds value*
> *and insight to their day.*

If you know there is the potential for business with a given contact, but you don't have any commitment for forward movement in the relationship, you *can't* simply call the person every day and ask, "Are we doing business together?" That's a waste of time and energy, and it tends to turn off prospects. However, what you can do—and *must* do—is find a way to call, say, once a week and propose a new and creative way to win a spot on that person's radar screen.

FROM THE FRONT LINES

Steve Bookbinder, our senior trainer, also sells for us. Steve has a unique strategy for reinvigorating contacts who have fallen behind in returning his calls. He calls it the "headhunter gambit."

His objective is to reconnect without *sounding* like the average salesperson calling back to reconnect. Basically, Steve is trying to avoid this kind of call:

> "You and I spoke three months ago and you said that
> I should get back in touch today, and, well here I am
> getting in touch." (Awkward pause.) "So, what's up?"

To distinguish himself from the abysmal phone manners and business relationship management skills of the vast majority of salespeople out there, Steve takes advantage of the fact that he has been the target of a number of headhunters over the years. (Fortunately, for me, he always turns them down!)

Invariably, Steve's conversations with headhunters close with a request like this: "If you ever run into anyone who would be interested in a position like this, please be sure to have them give me a call at 212-555-5555."

How, you may ask, does such a request turn into a new way to wake up a dormant prospect or a dormant lead? Here's how.

Instead of calling up a contact and badgering the person about an unreturned phone call, a proposal he hasn't gotten feedback on, or a time line for later connection, Steve will leave a message something like this:

> "Hi, Jack. Steve Bookbinder from D.E.I. I just wanted to get in touch with you and let you know I got an interesting call that you are going to want to hear about. Give me a call when you can at 800-224-2140."

When the intrigued prospect calls back, as he or she almost always will, my trainer passes along the headhunting lead and suggests that if the contact knows of anyone within the desired hiring field, he or she might want to think about calling the number. The lead isn't an exact match with the prospect's background—which is probably good. The point is, Steve is calling to pass along a lead, not to pester about an unreturned call.

In virtually all of the cases, the person Steve is calling will bring up the fact that he or she owes my trainer a call, and the two of them will begin to talk about what has to happen next for the two companies to do business together!

I'm not suggesting that you must find a headhunter in order to reawaken relationships with dormant contacts. I am, however, suggesting that you take advantage of some of the countless ways you can call a dormant lead about something other than the fact that he or she hasn't called you back.

Telling people they haven't called you back just makes them defensive. Don't build your call around the other person's failure to keep in touch or failure to keep a commitment with you.

There are other ways to deal with a contact who isn't yet playing ball with you. One of my favorites is sending along books and articles. Over the years, I must have sent out tens of thousands of dollars worth of articles and books to prospects and customers. It seems, from a distance, like a hefty expense. But you have to view that expense in context!

I know for a fact that I've generated literally millions of dollars worth of sales by being able to get through to leads at extremely large companies because the CEO of the organization remembered me as the person who had sent along that interesting article. The beauty of this system, of course, is that I'm able to begin my conversation with something other than an appeal to rectify the past sin of not returning my calls. Instead, the contact and I can focus on the content of the book or article, and then, of course, discuss the possibility of my swinging by to meet the person face to face.

Here's another strategy you can use with a dormant account: the "wrong proposal" call. Let's say you've spent a fair amount of time putting together a proposal for a contact, and then heard nothing back. You can't get a meeting. You can't get a phone call. You have no Next Step. You're not getting any feedback. What do you do?

Instead of calling and saying, "You're not giving me the feedback I need," assume there's something wrong with the proposal you set up. It's a fair assumption, because action from the prospect is the only reliable sign of interest and buy-in, and you're not getting any action from this person. So you need to find a way to get interest and buy-in with a revised proposal.

Here's how you do that. Call the person up and say, "Marilyn, I've been thinking about what I put together for you, and I realized last night that it really doesn't match what you're doing. I've got an idea for another approach that I want to run past you. Can we get together tomorrow at 3:00 so I can show you some of the things I'm thinking about?" Or, "Marilyn, I've been looking at the proposal I gave you, and I think the pricing is wrong. Can we get together tomorrow at 9:00 so I can show you some new ideas?"

Only two things can happen from a call like that: either you'll get a Next Step or you won't. But you won't be on the fence!

Again: Sales don't just happen; we have to take the initiative to make them happen. We have to propose something that can't possibly be ignored—something that requires the person we're interacting with to respond to us. If he or she does respond to us, then we are, by definition, talking to a prospect—someone on which we should be focusing closely. If the person doesn't respond to us, then our contact cannot be classified as a prospect.

POINTS TO PONDER

- Consider using some variation on the "headhunter gambit."

- Find a way to call about something other than the fact that the person hasn't called you back.

- Assume there's something wrong with the plan you put together; call and suggest a meeting so you can go over the new ideas you've come up with.

CHAPTER 13

...in which we learn how to move up the ladder

"By asking for the impossible, attain the best possible."

—ITALIAN PROVERB

*I*f you know for certain that your contact cannot make the decision or get the decision made for you, you must tactfully ask a technical or logistical question that your prospect will not be able to answer, but that the true decision maker would be able to answer.

When the prospect says, "I don't know," you can say something like this: "Well, that's actually going to be pretty important. Do you know who we could talk to about that?"

This is an excellent way to move up the ladder with your contact. You move up the ladder by posing a question that is impossible to ignore, but that the prospect will be motivated to help you answer.

FROM THE FRONT LINES

When we're dealing with a large account, we may ask a question like this: "How long does the consumer usually have to wait for delivery once the order has been entered into the computer system?"

The person we're talking to won't have this information, but the decision maker we're targeting will. So we ask detailed questions in a specific area and then try to build alliances that will help us connect with the people who can answer our questions.

Don't be misled by titles or organizational charts. Titles can be extremely misleading. A person can have the most impressive title in the world, but have literally no knowledge about the area of activity that title suggests. (For instance, a media relations officer may have little or no talent for dealing with editors working under tight deadlines.)

Look past the title and the formal organizational structure, and use effective questioning to get your contact to identify the people who have the actual power to make things happen for you. Then say, "You and I really should arrange for a meeting with so-and-so. Could we try to set something up for Monday afternoon of next week? How's 2:00?" Or: "You should really be meeting with our senior vice president. I'd like to bring him in next week to talk to you and your boss. Could we set something up for Wednesday at 1:00?"

Another strategy for extending your network within a sale is simply to make noise at another level, regardless of what you may or may not have heard from your contact in the past. I only recommend this in those situations where you are absolutely stymied and cannot make the sale happen any other way, because, technically, you are going over the contact's head. Still, there are some times when making noise at another level makes sense, especially when you are dealing with bureaucratic or hierarchical obstacles that have a lot to with turf issues and very little to do with actual performance on the field.

If you do decide to pull what is popularly known as an "end run" around some contact who seems to be deliberately roadblocking you, the best way to do it may well be to send your outline, proposal, or other materials—via snail mail or e-mail—to the contact you want to bring into discussion (say, the president of the organization). In that case, you can get around the wrong person simply by selling higher up with an apology that reads as follows:

> I'm sorry I didn't include you on this in the first place. I'd be eager to get your comments on what we put together so far.

Alternatively, you can copy everyone with your message, although doing that can get complicated sometimes.

Admittedly, going over someone's head is probably not the not the best way to make allies within an organization if you've already built up a powerful alliance with someone. But in a situation where you have absolutely nothing to lose, and you have the choice between throwing the ball and failing to do so, it's better to do something that gets a response.

POINTS TO PONDER

- Prepare a question that only the decision maker you're targeting could answer.

- Pose that question to your contact.

- Suggest a specific time and date for a meeting with you, your contact, and the person who can answer your question.

- Monitor what happens next. What is the response?

- Be ready to reach out independently to others in the organization if you have absolutely nothing to lose by doing so.

CHAPTER 14

...in which we learn the advantage of being righted

"Give me a good fruitful error any time, full of seeds, bursting with its own corrections. You can keep your sterile truth for yourself."

—VILFREDO PARETO

*T*he opposite of wrong is right and the opposite of right is wrong. That may seem self-evident, but look at what that simple idea actually means in practice: We don't have to be right in sales all the time. We simply need to be "righted."

Gathering the right information is impossible if we're concerned about not making a mistake in front of the prospect. Instead of assuming we're right, we must throw out the ball to the prospect by stating our assumptions about the situation in the hope of being corrected.

We have to restate what we've learned from the other person in a way that he or she can't ignore. Often, we have to suggest some kind of Next Step that would arise naturally from what we've learned. The person will then either correct us or agree to the Next Step. Obviously, if the person moves forward to the Next Step with us, we've confirmed our information, and we've still got an active prospect—someone to whom we're justified in devoting our ongoing time and attention.

FROM THE FRONT LINES

One day while making a presentation to a prospect, I found myself in a familiar position. I knew that the person I was speaking to was talking to another sales training company, but I didn't know which.

In years past, I had dealt with this situation, by doing what most people do, asking outright, "With whom are you working?" or "What other sales training firms are you talking to?"

The problem is that a good percentage of the time, many prospects, especially new prospects, will greet this request with a stony, "I'm afraid I can't tell you." Having been dealt this conversation-crippling blow dozens, if not hundreds, of times in the past, I decided to try something new with this organization. Instead of asking, "To whom are you talking?" I made a statement.

What I said was, "So, I'm assuming that we're the only sales training company you're talking to."

What happened next was remarkable. Whereas in many other situations I found that my information would be limited or nonexistent after posing a direct question ("What other sales organizations are you talking to?"), I found that this time my prospect was more than willing to correct me. I had made a statement that was factually incorrect and I listened in amazement as my contact with the company "straightened me out."

"Actually, Steve, we are talking to XYZ training company, ABC training company, and 123 training company as well. We are using a couple of different strategies to distinguish the vendors."

And on he went. By making a simple statement and allowing the prospect to correct me, I had thrown out the ball and unloosed a torrent of information. That information ended up helping us to secure what ended up being a very large sale indeed.

The principle is simple. Throw a fact on the table and wait for other people to correct it. This is a vitally important sales idea—one that has been neglected by far too many salespeople.

The only way that we can end up making a proposal that makes sense is by verifying what actually does make sense to this person in this situation. The only way you can do that is to throw out an idea and encourage the other person to correct you.

> *Salesperson:* "So, I'm assuming you want the training to start this quarter." (Stop talking.)
>
> *Prospect:* "Oh, no. We didn't want the training to start this quarter. It's supposed to start next quarter."
>
> *Salesperson:* "So—It looks to me like we're talking about training about 250 people." (Stop talking.)
>
> *Prospect:* "Oh, no. It's actually closer to 400 people."

People love to correct you. Put that principle to work in your selling process. Throw out a fact and see what kind of corrections come your way. If you don't confirm your assumptions, you can't develop the right plan—the plan that makes sense to the other person—and you won't close the sale!

POINTS TO PONDER

- Rather than simply asking for information, we also have to be willing to make a statement and let the prospect or customer correct our assumptions.

- We must be willing to be righted, because being righted is the only way we can ever make sure the plan is right.

- If we don't set up a proposal or plan that is right, we are not going to close the sale!

CHAPTER 15

...in which we learn what to do when the person won't give us the Next Step we want

"To believe it possible we may be in error, is the first step toward getting out of it."

—JOHANN K. LAVATER

Horrors! The prospect won't agree to the Next Step you've proposed.

Don't worry. All is not lost, as long as you're willing to assume personal responsibility and ask the prospect a question that is virtually impossible to sidestep. In the vast majority of situations, that question will show you exactly where you stand.

FROM THE FRONT LINES

Here's what we say when someone doesn't agree to the Next Step we've suggested:

"I'm genuinely surprised to hear you say that. Based on what we talked about today—A, B, and C—I really

would have thought we'd be ready to move forward.
Did I do something wrong?"

This question will uncover why your prospect is not willing
to agree to the Next Step you've proposed. (And by the way, if
you've done the right work up front, you should be genuinely
surprised if the person doesn't agree to move forward with you.)

When you ask, "Did I do something wrong?" something
very interesting happens. In 99 percent of the cases, you'll find
that your prospect responds by saying something like this:

"Oh, no, it's nothing that you've done. The problem is
really on our end. You see, the thing is . . .

Once you've gotten the person to say "the thing is," you'll
be well on your way toward learning the relevant details of the
situation you face.

In our experience, one of the very best ways to elicit facts is
to take responsibility. Be willing to say, "I'm sorry. Did I do
something wrong?" Then listen to the answer you get from the
prospect. If there's real opportunity here, you'll know about it in
short order. If there's not, you'll know that too, and you can
avoid spending more of your valuable time and energy on this
opportunity.

A side note: If you're not comfortable asking, "Did I do
something wrong?" you can also say this: "I'm really surprised.
When a meeting goes as well as this one did, usually people are
eager to move forward. I'm just curious, why wouldn't you want
to let me talk to your staff?"

POINTS TO PONDER

- Accept responsibility.

- State your (genuine) surprise at the situation.

- Ask if you've done something wrong or ask why the person wouldn't want to move forward.

CHAPTER 16

... in which we learn to emphasize what we know, not what we show

"Oil your mind ... Strength alone will not do, as young people are apt to think."

—LORD CHESTERFIELD

*T*he point of any meeting with a prospect is to get specific feedback that supports a Next Step. This means that what most salespeople consider "objections" and "resistance" are actually very good signs. They show us that the prospect is willing to critique what we're suggesting should happen next in the relationship. That's information that can help us as we develop the right recommendation about what we think should happen next.

The worst outcome is not when the prospect tells us what we've proposed is wrong. The worst outcome is when the prospect says, "This is fascinating. Let me think about it."

Everything we do in the sales process must be geared toward emphasizing the unique information we've gathered about this particular prospect. If we get distracted by anything else—our message, our format, our priorities—we're in trouble.

FROM THE FRONT LINES

Several months before I started writing this book, I went on a meeting with one of our senior salespeople that bombed completely. On the ride back to the office, I realized what the problem was: I had allowed my sales rep to become seduced by her own technology. She had gotten distracted by the snazzy PowerPoint presentation, the four-color proposal document, the snazzy-looking pie charts. She'd had so much fun playing with her proposal-generation toys that she lost sight of the more important goal: finding out about what the other person was doing.

We'd made a critical mistake. We'd focused on what we were showing, not on unique information about this particular prospect. Our proposal looked great! But we didn't know enough about the other person for all that fancy presentation material to add up to anything in the prospect's mind. If my rep had spent half as much time asking good questions as she had tweaking colors on her proposal document, we might have gotten somewhere.

As it stood, though, we lost the deal.

Most of the salespeople I meet get distracted by their own selling tools. They get so excited about the chance to show off their fancy proposal that they don't ask themselves a basic question: What do I really know about this person and this organization?

The salespeople I'm talking about lose sight of the importance of being righted by the prospect, which is an essential prerequisite to being right. As a result, they spend most of their time preparing long-winded, fancy-looking proposals, laminates, and PowerPoint presentations that are so vague that they aren't—can't be—right from the prospect's point of view. Why not? Because the essential assumptions haven't been verified yet! Too often salespeople think of their written materials as finalizing tools, when they should be using them as verifying tools.

Consider these two selling sequences:

1. The first meeting leads to full-blown presentation with all the bells and whistles at the second meeting, which leads to a "Gee, let me think about it" response from the prospect.

2. The first meeting leads to an abbreviated two-page miniproposal listing key assumptions at the second meeting, which leads to the prospect scribbling all over the miniproposal at the second meeting, which leads to a "This looks great!" response from prospect at the third meeting.

Which would you prefer to see? I don't know about you, but I'll do just about anything to avoid closing the meeting with a "Gee, let me think about it" outcome.

In the first sequence, you're letting the materials drive the sale. In the second sequence, you're using the materials to provoke a reaction from the prospect. You're making noise! And when you do that, you can expect the prospect to make a little noise in return:

"Hold on a minute. This isn't what I had in mind. We were thinking in terms of something totally different. You see, the thing is . . ."

If your information hasn't been verified, no amount of flash will make your proposal make sense from the prospect's point of view.
As you've already learned, the words "the thing is" from a prospect are music to a good salesperson's ears. But, as a general rule, the only way you get to hear that music is by taking the initiative, drawing some conclusions, and being willing to be corrected before you make a formal presentation.

You can't get to "the thing is" if you're afraid of being corrected! And that's what your selling tools should do for you: give the prospect the opportunity to correct you. Don't fool yourself into thinking that a beautiful color document, or a slick brochure, or a snazzy PowerPoint presentation will do the work for us. Contrary to popular opinion, we can't know what the prospect is trying to accomplish from the first instant of the first meeting. The only way we can expect to find out what makes this person different from the last 30 or 50 or 90 we spoke to is to use our materials as verifying tools, not closing tools.

"Here are some of the assumptions I've made, based on what we talked about last time."

If you haven't yet used your written materials to help you make the noise that gets you righted, then you're wasting your time developing that multicolored proposal and that 36-slide animated PowerPoint show!

Think again of that sales rep with whom I went out on a meeting. Her materials looked fantastic, but they didn't match what the prospect wanted to do! Obviously, she hadn't verified her information. She hadn't gotten the prospect to scribble all over the one-page summary before she put together the detailed proposal. She'd never gotten the prospect to say, "Well, the thing is . . ."—at least, not before she made a formal recommendation. As a result, she lost the sale.

After the meeting, I shared with her the concepts I'm sharing with you in this chapter, namely: It isn't what you show, it's what you know that counts.

POINTS TO PONDER

- Use a brief, low-tech, miniproposal to get feedback from the prospect before you go all out with an in-depth presentation.

- Use written materials as verification tools.

- Always remember: The worst outcome is when the prospect says, "This is fascinating; let me think about it."

CHAPTER 17

…in which we learn the ultimate standard for finding out whether prospects have moved forward in the sales cycle with us

"Unless commitment is made, there are only promises and hopes—no plans."

—PETER F. DRUCKER

*D*oes it really make sense to make a formal recommendation that a given prospect should work with us?

We cannot really answer this question with a yes unless we have at least a clear sense of what the person is trying to do. When in doubt, focus on what the person is doing, has done, and is planning to do in the future, and how and why.

For instance: "How are you planing to increase sales over the next quarter? Why did you choose that approach?"

If you ask enough impossible-to-ignore questions like these, you'll eventually you'll find yourself in a position to share what your own organization does. Instead of launching into a preprogrammed, one-size-fits-all pitch, emphasize a single success story that is uniquely appropriate to this prospect. For instance:

"It's interesting you mention changing the responsibilities of your underwriters to include sales activity. We just finished putting together a program for Acme Insurance that helped them make just that kind of transition with their underwriters. What we found was. . . ."

Many people treat selling as though it were something that's very complex. Actually, selling is simply a matter of finding out what makes sense to the other person. If you do that, closing the sale is simply a matter of saying, "It makes sense to me. What do you think?"

Sometimes salespeople ask, "How do I know whether or not what I'm proposing makes sense?" The answer is actually very simple. If the prospect begins to act as though closing the sale is as important to him or her as it is to you, it definitely makes sense! That's the ultimate standard for evaluating prospects who have moved through the sales process with you.

FROM THE FRONT LINES

Here are five questions I ask my own salespeople that help them focus on when not to deliver a formal recommendation to a prospect. By delivering fewer formal proposals than most other sales training companies, and by closely customizing the proposals we do deliver to people who are in fact interested in working through the steps of the sales cycle with us, we have been able to streamline our selling process. Your company can do the same thing:

1. Before you make a presentation, ask yourself: Am I sure I'm talking to the person who will be able to say yes? (Is there some other team member who will play a role?

How have other decisions like this been made in the past?) If you're not sure about this point, don't deliver the formal presentation.

2. Ask yourself: Am I sure this plan makes sense based on what I know this person is actually trying to do? Would I buy it? If the answer is no, don't deliver the formal presentation.

3. Ask yourself: Have I discussed all the relevant budget issues with my contact? Do the numbers make sense to him or her? (Raise the issue yourself—don't wait for the prospect to do so.) If the answer is no, don't deliver the formal presentation.

4. Ask yourself: Have I established a realistic timetable? If the answer is no, don't deliver the formal presentation.

5. Ask yourself: Does my contact know I expect to close this deal? Again: If you have any doubt, say something like this: "I'm going to gather everything we've done into a formal proposal for our meeting next Tuesday, and at that point, I don't see any reason why we wouldn't be able to finalize this." See what happens! If the contact does not know that you plan to close the sale, then you are not ready to make a formal presentation.

Remember: Sales don't just happen. They happen as the result of a process in which we continually take the initiative to do something to which the other person must respond. If the response is positive, we can conclude that we're justified in moving forward with that person in a given area.

POINTS TO PONDER

- Review the five presentation questions before you make any formal recommendation to a prospect.

- Ask yourself: What makes more sense—delivering 5 customized proposals to 5 prospects who really are playing ball with you, or delivering 25 uncustomized proposals that have little or nothing to do with what people are trying to accomplish?

CHAPTER 18

...in which we learn why it's important to de-emphasize "prospects" who exceed our typical selling cycle

"Time is a great teacher. Unfortunately, it kills all its pupils."

—HECTOR LOUIS BERLIOZ

*A*big, and common, problem in selling has to do with a failure to understand one's own selling cycle. We get caught in the "pending trap."

Let's say it typically takes us eight weeks to move from first contact to a completed sale. Suppose we find ourselves talking to a prospect who's in his twelfth week of discussion with us. Or suppose we find ourselves dealing with a lot of people who have significantly exceeded the average amount of time it takes us to close a sale. What does that mean?

It means we're wasting time. Salespeople don't like to admit that, but it's true. Even with a potentially big account. Even with a great relationship. Even with every "green light" in the world flashing. If a prospect significantly exceeds your average selling cycle and you continue to spend time on the prospect, you run the risk of being in permanent "pending" mode. If every prospect you interact with exceeds your selling cycle, you've fallen into the pending trap. Nothing's closing; everything's on hold; you're wasting your time. And time is something you can't get back.

Sales don't just happen. We have to take action in a direct, impossible-to-ignore way, and propose a clear course of action. At some point, that course of action has to sound like this: "You know what? This really makes sense to me. I think we should get started. Does it make sense to you?" If the person responds positively to our suggestion, we know he or she is really interested in working with us. If the person doesn't respond appropriately, we have to move on, or at least commit to spend our time with people who are working within a more realistic time frame.

It's a statistical fact: Prospects who exceed your average selling cycle become steadily less likely to buy as time passes. Make intelligent choices about individual prospects, but don't spend all your time pursuing a lead that has been pending for twice the length of your cycle!

You must know the typical amount of time it takes you to close a sale.

Every selling environment has an average selling cycle. By identifying yours and tracking which prospects have significantly exceeded your cycle, you can manage your time more effectively.

If that period is 60 days, then every time a prospect remains pending beyond 60 days, your odds of selling to that person decrease! Schedule accordingly.

FROM THE FRONT LINES

A few years back, I got talked into going on a fourth appointment to a "major account" that had not made a commitment to us.

Let me explain: At this stage of my company's growth, I usually come in to meet with the top management of an organization once. Maybe twice. If things are unusually complicated, I'll reconnect with the management team or the target company's training team before we close the deal. Members of my sales team, of course, may have many more meetings than that; I'm just tracking my own involvement in our organization's sales process here.

Here's my point: Over the years, I've developed an understanding of my role in our company's selling cycle. If something's going to happen, it happens by the end of the second meeting in which I take part.

Three meetings before we get any kind of purchase commitment? There's a major problem somewhere.

Four meetings? Unless there's some kind of divine intervention, a deal is out of the question.

Now, I knew this. Yet on the occasion of which I'm speaking, with this "huge potential account," I was persuaded to make not my first, not my second, not even my third trip to the client's headquarters; a member of our sales team talked me into making the fourth visit. This was on the theory that this visit would be the one that straightened out all the problems, confirmed the right information, and set us up to close the deal.

It didn't.

I should have known it wouldn't because in these situations, I've learned from bitter experience. The odds of the organization actually taking action and buying from us are virtually nonexistent. After three visits from me, there's more than enough information on both sides to figure out whether or not something's going to happen. A fourth visit is confirmation that we're in the permanent pending phase. And that's precisely where we were. We did not get that deal.

Please understand: I want to be involved in the selling efforts of my people. In fact, I require them to build me into their selling process. But I also know my selling cycle. And the next time someone asks me to go meet with the same people for the fourth time, I'm going to check the calendar and see whether or not it's April Fool's day, because at this point everyone in my organization knows better than to ignore our company's selling cycle.

The passage of time without positive action from the prospect can kill deals. Don't pretend it can't.

POINTS TO PONDER

- Know your average selling cycle.

- Know when to disengage from "prospects" who significantly exceed your average selling cycle.

- If you haven't gotten a commitment from a prospect who's spent too long in the pending category, think hard about whether you should still be giving a commitment.

- Understand that the simple passage of time can kill a sale.

CHAPTER 19

...in which we learn why it's important to take it personally when you lose a deal to the competition

"Thank God for competition. When our competitors upset our plans or outdo our designs, they open infinite possibilities of our own work to us."

—GIL ATKINSON

I was working with a manager a couple of days ago on a training program. I listened as he told his reps "not to take it personally" when they lost a sale to a competitor. That's nonsense. You should take it personally. You should be poised and respond professionally, but you should definitely take it personally when a competitor steals your business.

If you don't take losing a big sale (or even a medium-sized sale) to a competitor personally, you may not get frustrated enough. You may not ever get motivated to ask yourself, "What am I doing wrong?" If you ask yourself that question honestly, you'll be led instantly to the next question, which is "What am I doing now that didn't match up with what that prospect was doing?"

If you take it personally, you're likely to ask those questions, and you'll be motivated to throw out the ball again in a way that the prospect you just "lost" can't possibly ignore. Some of the time—not all of the time, but some of the time—that will result in your actually winning the business back from your competitor.

FROM THE FRONT LINES

Let me give you an example of what I mean. We work with a huge data services company that has offices both in Europe and in the United States. We had done an extensive training program with this company in New York City. After we had been successful with that program, we made a point of taking the president of the company out to lunch the next time he visited New York. (This president, by the way, is based in Europe.)

At that meeting, we asked lots of questions about what the president was trying to accomplish, who his target markets were in Europe, what his strategy was for reaching those markets, and so on. Again, we did this even after we had completed the program successfully in New York. It never makes sense to stop asking what we call "do-based" questions. As you've probably gathered, these are questions that focus on what the other person is doing, hopes to do, or has done in the past.

As we had hoped, we soon got a call from the European office of this customer of ours. They wanted us to come in and make a proposal to do an extensive series of training programs in Europe. So we did some phone interviews, traveled overseas, made our presentation, and felt very good about how things went.

Not long after we got back to the States, however, we received a letter from someone from the target company whom we had never heard of before informing us that we had not gotten the significantly larger piece of business from our current customer. One of the other companies we had been competing against won the account. At that stage, we didn't know which company we lost the business to.

Well, I took that personally. We put a lot of work into that account. So I came up with an idea. We were still doing a program for that same company in New York City. I picked up the phone and offered to fly the president of the company from Europe out to New York to see exactly how we were training his staff in the New York City office. He had never seen us in action!

Talk about an impossible-to-ignore Next Step!

Notice what I didn't do. I didn't call the president back and say, "Gee, we're disappointed with your decision." Nor did I call him up and say, "Please reverse your decision." I called him up and asked him what he thought had happened. As I suspected, he had no idea. Someone else in the organization had come down against us; he was mystified. I then asked him to take a specific course of action. I asked him to get on a plane at my expense, come out and take a look at the training work we were doing, and let me know whether or not our program was still in keeping with what he was trying to accomplish during that fiscal year.

When I made that offer, he had to do something. My suggestion was on the table. Did he want a free ticket to New York City or didn't he?

The president accepted my offer, and to my great satisfaction the strategy worked. The president loved our program and reversed the decision. We trained his company in Europe, thereby winning a much bigger piece of business than we previously had in New York City. The company now stands as one of our best customers.

Let me leave you with another important point about the way we rescued that sale. We didn't turn the entire office upside down and completely reorient our schedule toward rescuing this sale. We simply made noise within the account, based on what we already knew this customer was trying to accomplish! Specifically, we did not neglect the development of new business. We took ten minutes, tops, to figure out a strategy of how to resurrect the account, thinking about what kind of unignorable request, statement, or suggestion we could make to this contact. Then I picked up the phone.

Can you imagine what would have happened in this situation if I had simply sent along a thank-you-for-considering-us letter and not made that phone call?

I feel very strongly about losing business to the competition. I take it personally. I figure out a question I can ask, and I focus on what I know the other person is trying to do. My viewpoint is that if I've already put together a proposal of some kind, and I'm actively talking about pricing and timing, and I'm dealing with the right decision maker—if I get the sale to that level— and the decision does not go my way, then I take it personally. I don't blow out my schedule, but I do try to find some way to reconnect with my decision maker and throw out the ball one more time.

POINTS TO PONDER

- Take it personally when you lose a deal to the competition.

- If you've worked together with the prospect to develop a proposal that really does make sense, but you lose the business, call the decision maker yourself and throw out the ball one more time.

CHAPTER 20

...in which we learn to raise the tough issues ourselves

"People of genius whenever they are faced with misfortune find resources within themselves."

—BROUHOURS

*D*on't run from your intuition about what's happening in the sale. Trust it. Raise the tough issues yourself. Don't wait for the prospect to raise them!

If you want to find out where things really stand, tell the truth as you see it and see what happens. Do something that's absolutely impossible for the other person to ignore. Then stop talking and gauge the other person's reaction. If you get a positive response, you've still got forward movement in the relationship. If you don't, you know where the work lies.

Prospects are shocked when you say things like, "I'm concerned that your people aren't really ready to work with us to put this together." But once you do say that, you'll either have an ally in the organization, or you'll be free to put this deal to rest and move on to something else.

Put your own experience to work. Raise potential problem areas on your own.

FROM THE FRONT LINES

Recently I met with a prospect who had fewer salespeople in his organization than we typically train.

This was not the first time I've met with such a prospect. In fact, over the years, I've probably held hundreds upon hundreds of meetings with CEOs of such companies. They've heard about our results with larger organizations, and they decide to call me and set up a meeting. Just about anyone who comes out and asks me directly for a meeting will get one, so I end up meeting with the heads of a lot of companies who are smaller than the ones we would typically target through our own cold calling work.

So here's a situation I've been in countless times. And I've noticed a pattern: Our pricing is sometimes an obstacle. Now, I really can anticipate and prepare for that response. It's just a question of how effectively I'm going to do that.

Given that I know there's a statistical likelihood for this kind of prospect to react with a certain panicked silence when he learns about our pricing structure, what should I do? I don't want to assume that this company is exactly like all the other companies I've ever met with; that's not fair to the prospect, and it's not fair to my company either. So I won't come out and say, "I really don't think you can afford to work with us," at the beginning of the meeting. Who knows? I could be wrong!

By the same token, though, I don't really want to spend an hour of my day gathering information from this contact if the pricing issue is eventually going to keep us from working together. I want us to reach a mutual conclusion about my intuition that there might be a difficulty with pricing. So, how could

I structure the meeting in such a way as to respect this prospect's uniqueness, but still retain control of the exchange? In other words, how could I get each of us the best information as quickly as possible?

Here's what I did. Once the prospect and I had passed the small talk section of the meeting, I asked, "Would it help if I told you a little bit about us and about what we do?" (This is an invaluable "getting down to business" question, by the way. We have trained salespeople all over the world to use it to focus the initial part of the meeting.)

After the prospect said, "Sure," which is what virtually always happens, I gave a brief, three-or-four-sentence summary of my company's history. It's absolutely essential that this description be a brief one. I'm certainly not out to make any kind of recommendation or deliver a long monologue at this stage of the relationship!

After my condensed summary of what D.E.I. was all about, I immediately asked a question that focused on something that we do, but phrased from the prospect's point of view. In this case, I asked, "Just out of curiosity, have you ever worked with a sales training company before?"

The prospect told me that he hadn't.

Then I asked another question: "What made you decide to get in touch with us?" Notice that I began with a short summary of D.E.I., but was, in just over a minute, fully engaged in the information-gathering portion of the sales relationship. I was trying to find out what had changed in the prospect's world to motivate him to call us.

What has changed? Be ready to ask, in a direct and impossible-to-ignore way, about the prospect's past, present, and future operations. Ask "how" and "why" questions as the information-gathering step unfolds. It's particularly impor-

tant to find out what has recently changed in the prospect's situation.

I learned that the prospect was eager to take advantage of a startling new technological advance within his company, and that he hoped to use training to help increase the odds that his small sales team would deliver a successful product launch. If they did, he was certain he could take his company from low-level player to one of the industry leaders.

By this point, I'd gathered just enough information to know that there could be a chance to deliver value for this company, assuming that the pricing issue could be made to work for both sides. But I still had my "gut instinct" feeling that pricing was eventually going to be a challenge with this prospect. So here's what I did: Instead of waiting to step on that particular booby trap after another month, or another week, or even another hour of discussions with this contact, I set it off myself.

At this early stage of the discussion, only a few minutes or so into the meeting, I raised the tough issue myself—but from a safe position. Here's how I did it: I simply said, "I have to tell you, before we go any further, I'm concerned about something."

Then I stopped talking.

The prospect said, "Really? What are you concerned about?"

I said, "Well, I can see how we might be able to add value in the situation you've described, but, frankly, our pricing structure is designed for a lot larger sales force."

He said, "How much do you think a program like this is likely to cost?"

I gave him a rough estimate. I told him that I thought it would probably fall between X and Y per day of training. In doing so, I was making noise. The prospect had to react some-how. If he fell off the sofa and gasped for air, I could be fairly sure that the pricing I'd mentioned wasn't likely to work. If he nodded, maintained eye contact, and responded positively, I could be fairly sure that the relationship was indeed worth more time and effort.

As it happened, this prospect nodded, maintained eye contact, and told me that neither he nor his investors would be likely to have a problem with a fee in the range I'd described. We eventually closed the sale.

The point is not that you should always say you're concerned about pricing during the first meeting. (I do have a few salespeople, though, who make a point of raising price issues very early on in the relationship, and it seems to work for them.) The point is that you must be ready to identify and raise problem issues yourself, before the prospect does and before the formal presentation.

That having been said, let me mention that, as a practical matter, I encourage salespeople never to attempt to close a sale before they've raised a specific dollar amount and gotten the prospect's reaction to it.

Why wait for six weeks or longer to discuss pricing? Why give the prospect the opportunity to say, "Gee, the price seems a little high to me?" when you could have had that discussion a month and a half ago?

Why extend your sales cycle by giving the prospect an excuse to say, "Gee, I'll have to think about it?"

Find out what's going on in the sale! And do so as early as you can.

Look at this principle again in another setting, one where we're visiting the prospect for the second time. Here's what we might say:

"Here's an outline of what our formal proposal might look like. Based on what you told me last time, these would be my assumptions. Based on those assumptions, this is what I'd probably recommend. And here's what we would charge for that program. And here's what the time line would look like. Before we put together a full proposal, though, I want to see what you think of what we've done so far. How does it look to you?"

Then stop talking!

Throw out the ball. The other person has to react somehow. Wait for the reaction. Will the ball come back? Will it drop to the floor? Will the other person catch it and hold on to it for dear life?

Whatever the prospect does in response to your question will tell you where you stand. You can raise any difficult issue in this way—before delivering your formal proposal—and deal with the big issues sooner, rather than later.

Once you raise the difficult issue—whether it's pricing, timing, payment terms, personnel, or anything else—monitor the other person's body language and tonality as well as his or her words. If I raise price, and I notice a sudden tension in the person's body language and an abrupt change in tone, then the prospect has already "told" me that what I'm proposing won't work, whether or not those exact words leave the person's mouth.

To get to the bottom of why what I'm proposing won't work as it's currently set out, I might have to give the prospect overt permission to open up to me. One way to do that is to say, "You know, if people have a problem with price (or timing, or program focus, or anything else), it usually comes up at this part of the meeting. How does this look to you?"

And then, having made some noise in an impossible-to-ignore way about the problem area, I would stop talking and wait patiently to see what happens next.

We usually get closer to the right deal, not further away from it, when we raise tough issues early. If we get further away, it's because there really was no deal to begin with, and that's worth knowing before you invest your time and energy on a given lead!

POINTS TO PONDER

- Listen to your instincts.

- Raise tough issues yourself, and do so early.

- If your experience tells you that there's a potential obstacle to the deal, or a problem with the proposal, raise it with the prospect now. Don't wait a month or more.

- Specifically, be sure you have clarified all pricing concerns before you deliver a formal recommendation.

CHAPTER 21

...in which we call in the cavalry

"The way a team plays as a whole determines its success. You may have the greatest bunch of individual stars in the world, but if they don't play together, the club won't be worth a dime."

—BABE RUTH

One of the issues we sometimes come up against in delivering our training programs has to do with the notion of bringing in management as a way of getting a response from the prospect. Sometimes the companies we work with say, "We've never done that before. The way we've always worked is the salesperson sells and the manager manages. Why should we change things around and have the salesperson use the manager as a means of escalating the sales?"

The answer we give is: Because it works. And that pretty much settles the argument.

Bringing in management shakes up the status quo, sets up impossible-to-ignore Next Steps, and shows you exactly where you stand with the prospect. The most successful salespeople in our organization all use senior management to move sales forward, close deals, confirm interest, and pull deals out of the fire. We don't care. We do everything they ask us to do, and we smile when we sign the commission checks.

The companies we train who follow our example with regard to management involvement post better sales totals than the companies who don't. That's enough for us, and it should be enough for your manager. If your manager has any doubts on the matter, share this book with him or her or have your manager call us directly so we can explain the strategy in full!

FROM THE FRONT LINES

A few years back, one of our sales representatives was on the verge of closing a major sale with a Canadian bank. I knew that this sale was on the verge of closing because I keep in close contact with each and every potential sale over a certain dollar amount.

When the word came through that the sale had not gone our way, I decided to try to rescue the sale. To make this strategy work, your management team must be ready to get involved. The idea is not to grovel, but to do whatever it takes to get back on the prospect's radar screen and get the right information—in a hurry.

In this case, I checked in on behalf of our sales rep, got in contact with the person with whom he'd been speaking, and said something like the following:

> "I heard from Gino today that you decided not to work with us on the program for March of this year. I really didn't anticipate that that would happen because it sounded to me like everything was going along very well and that Gino had been doing a good job. Clearly,

though, he seems to have gone wrong somewhere. So I am just calling to find out where Gino went wrong. I would really appreciate it if you could tell me what happened."

(By the way, Gino didn't care what I had to say to the prospect to get the deal back on track, and you shouldn't care either.)

That's the way I started the conversation with the contact. Working together, Gino and I were able to set up a new meeting, restructure the program, and save the deal. In that case, I was lucky enough to get through to the person directly. If I had been in a situation where I had to leave a voice mail message, I would have left a message within minutes of having heard that there was a problem with the sale. The message would have sounded something like this:

> "Hi this is Steve Shiffman calling with regards to Gino Sette. I need to talk to you as soon as you can, please call me at 212-581-7390. Again, the number is 212-581-7390."

These messages have a way of getting returned in a hurry. I think the contact feels concerned for the salesperson he or she has just ditched, and perhaps just a little guilty about turning away after the person's put in all that work.

In any event, the idea is to get connected with the person who made the decision that went against your company as soon as possible and to do so in an impossible-to-ignore way, by means of bringing someone new into the picture. Ideally, the person who calls should be higher up organizationally, and should not have had any previous long-term contact with this decision maker.

The key point is to get someone in on the process who is new to the process or relatively new to this decision maker and ask the question directly and forthright: Where did we go wrong? You will be surprised at the information that you gather and the possibilities that arise after you pose this question.

So far in this chapter, I've shared this highly successful strategy for using your organization's management team to rescue the sale. I hope it's clear from the rest of this book, though, that you can and should use your manager and your organization's technical experts as resources throughout the sales process. Bringing in senior members of your team works as a means of generating a Next Step, as a way of showing your organization's concern for the prospect, and as a way of getting new information that you might not otherwise get. Let's face it: Bosses open up to other bosses in a way they sometimes don't open up to salespeople.

POINTS TO PONDER

- Use your boss or other senior members of the team to rescue seemingly "lost" sales.

- Use your boss or other senior members of the team to generate a Next Step, to show your organization's concern for the prospect, and as a way of getting new information that you might not otherwise get.

CHAPTER 22

...in which we learn how to tell prospects when they screw up

"I love fools' experiments. I am always making them."

—CHARLES DARWIN

H ere's an interesting and all-too-infrequently employed variation on the "stop 'em in their tracks" approach to rescuing a sale. It's probably the most direct strategy for doing something impossible to ignore and generating a response from the prospect that you'll learn about in this book. When and where you apply it is up to you.

FROM THE FRONT LINES

I'll share with you the most dramatic of the many situations where we have used this selling strategy to our advantage. Not long ago our vice president of training, Steve Bookbinder, had been in a series of discussions with a major prospect in the pharmaceutical industry for a series of training programs. He had several meetings with his contact at this company. Steve came back to the office one afternoon to find that the prospect had left him the kind of message that every salesperson dreads hearing. It went something like this:

> "Steve, thanks so much for your interest and advice to our company over the past several weeks. Unfortunately, we've decided to go with another approach and we are not now looking for any of the programs that your company offers. We are, however, interested in tracking down information about a negotiation program, which, unfortunately, D.E.I. does not provide. I'd appreciate it if you give me a call back with some information on a negotiation program that you feel would be right for our team. Many thanks, John Prospect, 212-555-5555."

After voicing a few choice expletives, most salespeople would have picked up the phone to either supply the referral name or plead for another meeting to make their case. Interestingly, though, Steve took another approach.

Steve decided to leave an equally striking voice mail message in response—a voice mail message designed to make the prospect stop, listen, and respond in some way, positive or negative, to what Steve had to say. It wasn't necessarily an easy message to leave, but it was quite effective, and it did rescue the sale, so I'm sharing it with you here. This is what Steve's message sounded like:

> "Hi, Mr. Prospect. This is Steve Bookbinder from D.E.I. Management Group. Thanks for your message. I appreciate your getting back in touch with us. I have to

say, though, that having met with the members of your team and talked to the various people on your staff, I can tell you with some certainty the negotiation program is absolutely the wrong program for your people and your situation. So although there are any number of people I could recommend who do negotiation programs, and there are some situations where a program like that would be appropriate, yours isn't one of them. I've talked with everyone at the Boston office and the Los Angeles office and the New York office, and all of my phone calls and my meetings with you indicate that what's happening with your team is that they're simply not prospecting effectively. That's why I think we ought to talk in more detail about the appointment making program that we offer, because what I've learned from your people points me toward the conclusion that they're not going to be able to negotiate anything until they start developing enough leads to close more business. So I hope you can call me soon at 800-224-2140 so that we can discuss the appointment making program. I'll be here in the New York office all day today and all day tomorrow. Again, the number is 800-224-2140."

Not only did Steve receive a call back, he ultimately closed that deal. His highly confident, information-based voice mail message would not have worked if he had not done the necessary research up front to convey a professional recommendation of detail and authority. It also helped that he didn't lose his cool on the phone, and that he made absolutely clear what he wanted to happen next in the sale.

As it happened, he was in a perfect position to stop the prospect in his tracks by saying, in essence, "You screwed up."

POINTS TO PONDER

- If you've got the research, the product or service, the unique prospect information, and the chutzpah to back it up, consider using the "you screwed up" strategy.

- Be sure you identify a clear Next Step when you do so.

- Be sure you maintain a calm, professional demeanor when you do so.

CHAPTER 23

...in which we learn to use terminology that gets a positive response

"Language is a process of free creation. Its laws and principles are fixed, but the manner in which the principles of generation are used is free and infinitely varied. Even the interpretation and use of words involves a process of free creation."

—NOAM CHOMSKY

Having spent the better part of 30 years conducting meetings with prospects and customers, I've come to an important conclusion. No matter how carefully we may try to prepare, no matter how much Internet research we may conduct ahead of time, there are certain key words and phrases that people tend to respond to either very positively or very negatively. I've also learned that these words vary from person to person, and that you only learn them through personal interaction with someone.

This brings me to one of the difficulties of writing a book like this. There is always the risk of giving people the wrong impression, specifically, by encouraging their belief that there is a single magic incantation that they can use that will automatically yield a positive response from every person with whom they speak. This just isn't true. No script or dialogue or outline works in every situation, because each person we talk to is different.

The challenge is not to memorize a specific set of words and phrases that you can recite without thinking during every telephone call or a face-to-face meeting. The challenge is to notice what kind of response you get from an individual contact or prospect and how that response should drive what you have to say next.

When making noise, do so using terminology that resonates positively with the prospect.

FROM THE FRONT LINES

George Richardson, one of our senior salespeople, was engaged in serious discussions with a major high-tech firm about our training in prospect management. He noticed something strange, though, during the first meeting. Every time he used the word training with his contact, a strange, panicked look came over the person's face, and the atmosphere in the room instantly changed for the worse. It didn't take long for him to realize that he had a problem and that it had something to do with what this person had connected to the word training in his central nervous system.

From that point forward the sales rep decided that instead of speaking about a training program, he would instead start discussions by referencing our prospect management "workshop." Workshop, it turned out, got smiles and enthusiastic nods, whereas training always got ashen, tight-lipped stares.

So it was that we proposed a series of Next Steps about a prospect management workshop. That's what we ended up closing with that high-tech firm, a prospect management workshop, not a prospect management training session! Same content, same experience, different name. My point is, he built all his impossible-to-ignore Next Step proposals around the prospect's terminology, not around our terminology. If he'd focused on the words we were comfortable using, he never would have closed that sale.

We learned later that this particular company seems to have had a bad experience with another sales training organization, thereby leading not only to a negative feeling about one of our competitors, but about the whole notion of paying for "training"! A face-to-face workshop was what made sense for his organization and for ours.

The moral: Stay observant. Find out what terms the prospect reacts positively to; find out which words have negative connotations. Then find ways to minimize the use of words with negative connotations and find ways to work words and phrases with positive connotations into whatever Next Step you propose.

POINTS TO PONDER

- Be observant. Monitor the prospect's facial expressions and body language closely at all times.

- Stay away from words that obviously produce negative reactions in your prospect's world and, therefore, make it hard for him or her to commit to a Next Step.

- Find ways to adopt words that obviously produce positive reactions in your prospect's world and, therefore, make it easy for him or her to commit to a Next Step.

CHAPTER 24

...in which we learn how to find out where we really stand in the prospect's world

"Everyone lives by selling something."

—ROBERT LOUIS STEVENSON

I have a rule that I follow religiously. I never make a formal presentation when I know for certain that the person is not yet ready to give me the business. That may seem like common sense. Yet the vast majority of the salespeople we come in contact with walk into presentations having no idea how the prospect feels about what they're proposing.

That's not the way to succeed in sales. Before we attempt to close the sale, we must find out, by means of an impossible-to-ignore question, exactly where we stand in the prospect's world. Here's the best strategy for doing that.

FROM THE FRONT LINES

At the end of the meeting with a major wireless telecommunications firm, I shook my contact's hand and engaged in the lighthearted banter that usually signals the conclusion of the "business" part of the discussion. My contact, one of the senior executives in the organization, passed along a few jokes; I shared a couple of brief anecdotes that had nothing whatsoever to do with the training business we had been discussing for the past 90 minutes or so.

As we stood up, I reached over to shake my contact's hand and told him it had been a pleasure to meet with him that day. (I wasn't kidding him or misleading him; I really was glad that he and I had spent the time together that we had.) Then, before making my way back out to the reception area, I found out what was really going on in the sale.

I used the social ease of the situation to return, casually, to the "business" subject that had been the purpose of my entire trip that day. While my contact and I were still relaxed and comfortable with each other—still in our post-meeting mind-set—I said this:

"So tell me, Jack, just between you and me . . . what do
you think is really going to happen here?"

Then I stopped talking and waited to see what he would say in response.

By this point in the book, I hope you noticed that in posing such a question, I was throwing out the ball to my contact and waiting to see exactly what would come back. I was deliberately raising the tension in the relationship by posing an impossible-to-ignore question, one that was designed to deliver the best possible information about exactly what my contact's thinking was. But in increasing the tension, I wasn't making my contact tense. I was simply making use of the natural social interplay that takes place at the end of a business meeting. The question was completely appropriate to the moment; I didn't deliver it in a "hard sell" way at all.

Jack smiled and looked at me for a moment and then said, "Well, Steve, I have to tell you. I like what I've seen so far. If you can bring the final proposal in for under X amount, I think there is a very good chance we'll end up doing business together."

That was the information I wanted. I got it. We closed the deal the next week.

In a way, you could say that I had spent the entire 90-minute meeting preparing for the "casual" portion of the discussion to begin. You could say that I executed the "business" portion of the meeting well enough to use it as a springboard for the question in which I was really interested!

POINTS TO PONDER

- Never try to close a deal when you know for certain that the person isn't ready to give you the business.

- To find out where you really stand, consider asking this question at the end of the meeting, after the "business" portion of the conversation: "Just between you and me, what do you think is going to happen here?"

CHAPTER 25

...in which we learn to close the sale

"Always tell the truth. It's easier to remember."

—MARK TWAIN

Over the years, I've drawn a good deal of attention for having developed a closing strategy that's far more effective than most of the "closing tricks" sales trainers waste time sharing with their trainees. I prefer to think of mine as a closing strategy—as opposed to a closing "trick"—because there is really nothing tricky about it. In this chapter of the book, I'll explain the difference between a closing trick and a closing strategy, share how I developed the strategy for which our company has become well known—and, with any luck, convince you to avoid closing tricks altogether, for the rest of your sales career.

A closing trick is something that we do or say that's designed to persuade someone to buy, without basing our appeal on any particular piece of information that we've gathered from that prospect. If you take a look at some of the closing tricks passed along in some of the best-selling sales books and programs out there, you'll find plenty of examples of manipulative maneuvers like the ones to which I'm referring—maneuvers that have little or nothing to do with anything we've learned from the prospect.

For instance, you'll find some sales trainers advocating that you make some sort of suggestion about when and where to buy from them, and then "ride out" the silence that follows, if there is one. After a nice long silence, you're supposed to say, "Well, my mother always told me that silence was consent, so let's get you started."

Another approach you'll find offered with a straight face by some sales trainers is the "roll the pen" trick. In the "roll the pen" approach, the salesperson is supposed to roll a pen across the desk to the prospect, point toward the contract that's sitting on the desk, and then say confidently, "Press hard. You're making three copies."

And I heard of a chain of fitness centers that actually trained its sales representatives to attempt to close people who had taken advantage of a free week of exercise at the center by using the following absurd closing trick. When the prospect didn't immediately sign up for a paid week of membership, the salesperson was supposed to pull an unopened box of doughnuts out from his or her desk, slap the box of doughnuts down on the desk, and pronounce, "Okay, why don't you take these. You might as well give up right now."

I think you'll agree with me that all of these examples do not attempt to build on any information we've developed with the prospect.

In this book, I've given you a number of tools meant to help you open up the relationship, maintain forward movement in the sales process, and elicit information in a direct and unapologetic style. The reason I've given you these tools is so that when you reach the right point in the relationship, you can then turn to the prospect and say something like:

> "You know what? This really makes sense to me. Does it make sense to you?"

If you've spent most of your time gathering information, your plan will actually make sense to the prospect. That means you won't need fancy closing tricks. Instead, you can simply say: "It makes sense to me. What do you think?"

This is the world's simplest—and most effective— closing technique. It assumes that you have gathered and verified correct information about what the prospect is doing and how you can help him or her do that better.

In effect, we believe that the only effective way to close a sale is to turn to the prospect and say, "It makes sense to me. What do you think?"

When we use this "makes sense to me" closing strategy, we're forcing the other person to react. It's like tossing a ball out to the prospect. He or she has to respond somehow. If the person catches the ball and tosses it back to us by saying, "Yes, it does make sense. When can we start?" then we know we've closed the sale. By the same token, the other person could also respond, "No, it doesn't make sense." Then we can ask, "Really? Why not?" Either way, we're going to get some kind of response. (Sound familiar? By this point, I hope it does!)

When people tell us why our suggested proposal doesn't make sense, they are actually telling us what is wrong and how to correct it.

Again, the opposite of wrong is right and the opposite of right is wrong. We don't have to be right in sales all the time; we simply need to be "righted." And the "makes sense to me" close is one of the very best ways to get righted.

That closing strategy, which is now well known within the sales training industry as the "makes sense" close, is predicated on the notion that you have developed a specific plan—or even better, gotten the prospect to correct your own plan and develop it with you.

Let me tell you how I first developed this closing strategy.

FROM THE FRONT LINES

The "makes sense" close was born over a quarter of a century ago; I was just beginning my career as a sales trainer. One of my very earliest prospects was the owner of a chain of jewelry stores in New York City.

After the end of our first meeting, I realized that I didn't have a good enough understanding of this man's business to offer a full proposal on how I could help his company or people increase sales. So, at the conclusion of the first meeting, I said, "You know what? Instead of offering you an outline right now, what I'd like to do is go and meet with each of the counter people at your stores and find out exactly what is going on from their point of view. Then I can come back next Tuesday at 2:00 and show you an outline that will give you my best thinking on how we will proceed from here."

In other words, I threw out the ball.

The owner said, "Okay, that makes sense." So I met with each of the people at the various stores and took some notes.

Tuesday at 2:00 PM rolled around, and I met with the president again and showed him the outline I put together. I detailed what I learned from the counter staff, what my assumptions were, and how I felt I might be able to add value. This outline took up only a single page, but it gave my contact enough information to revise and update.

He pulled out his pen and scribbled all over that sheet, refocusing my efforts and helping me to know exactly where I needed to go with my full-scale proposal. At the end of that meeting, I scheduled yet another meeting by saying, "What I think we should do now is develop a full-scale proposal that we could look at next Friday at 1:00."

In other words, I threw out the ball.

The owner said, "Okay, that makes sense."

At the next meeting, he reviewed a proposal that I had typed, but that the two of us had essentially written together. After I reviewed everything that we had done together, it was second nature for me to say, "You know what, this really makes sense to me to get started with this next week. What do you think? Does it make sense to you?"

In other words, I threw out the ball.

The owner said, "Okay, that makes sense."

The minute I asked "Does it make sense to you?" I realized from my contact's expression that he trusted me and respected the work I had done to get the proposal right. That was how we both concluded that it was time to begin a series of training programs for his people.

I share this story with you so that you can see clearly how different the "makes sense" close is from the other closing ideas you may hear about. In particular, I hope it's obvious how useless it would be for anyone to attempt to employ this kind of closing technique without having worked side by side with the prospect to develop a plan that truly does make sense.

The closing technique in which I have now trained hundreds of thousands of salespeople all across the globe is based not on intimidation, but on a request for affirmation that what we're doing really does make sense. Again: The beauty of the approach is that if there's something that we're proposing that doesn't make sense, the prospect will invariably tell us what doesn't seem logical to him or her!

When it comes time to close the sale, you'll know, and your prospect should know, too. Once you're certain that both of you do know that what you're talking about makes sense, use the strategy I've outlined here. You'll have taken the first step to building a meaningful business alliance—the kind of alliance that turns prospects into customers.

POINTS TO PONDER

- Build an outline or preliminary plan based on interviews with the prospect.

- Encourage the prospect to revise this short document and give personalized feedback.

- When you and the prospect are both certain that the plan really does make sense, throw out the ball by using the "makes sense" close.

- If the prospect tells you the plan doesn't make sense, listen carefully to find out why it doesn't.

CHAPTER 26

... in which we learn nine principles for positive change over time

"If you don't drive your business, you will be driven out of business."

—B.C. FORBES

*H*ere are nine key concepts—core principles—that will help you move toward making sales happen, continuously and instinctively, in your daily activity. If you focus on them regularly, I think you'll find yourself growing as a sales professional over the long term.

1. *Understand the definition of selling.* The definition of selling is asking people what they do, how they do it, where they do it, when they do it, with whom they do it, and why they do it that way—and then, and only then, asking how we can help them do it better.

2. *Information is everything.* The information you gather is always the final determinant of the quality of your rela-

tionship with a prospect or customer. Where you are in the relationship always depends on the quality of the information you have gathered. If you do a better job of gathering and confirming information than anyone else, then you will build better relationships with customers and prospects than anyone else, and you will manage those relationships more effectively than anyone else.

3. *You must know what Next Step you're trying to close.* You're always closing something, even if you're not closing the sale yet. Your goal in selling is simply to get the other person's agreement to proceed with you to the Next Step. By finding out what the other person does, and focusing on whether or not the Next Step you're proposing makes sense, you make the eventual "makes sense" closing technique possible.

4. *Selling is more than a numbers game.* Many salespeople will tell you, "Selling is simply a numbers game." Supposedly, all you have to do is call enough people and you'll be successful. The truth is, though, that success in selling requires much more than simply piling up the numbers. You must understand your ratios and know how to monitor and improve them. By monitoring your activity ratios—dials to completed calls, completed calls to appointments, appointments to visits, and visits to sales—you can identify problem areas and improve your performance over time. Every portion of your sales activity exists in relation to some other part of that activity. If you know what your calls-to-discussions ratio is, you can develop strategies and goals that will help you improve that ratio. If you don't know your calls-to-discussions ratio, you won't be able to tell whether what you're doing is bringing you closer to your income goal!

5. *The first half of the success equation in sales is energy.* Early on in the process of building a business relationship, it takes energy to get onto the person's radar screen and stay there long enough to get the necessary information. If you have the necessary energy, and make the right number of initial contacts with people, you'll do all right. However, you won't necessarily be performing at the peak level. (See Principle 6.)

6. *The second half of the success equation in sales is intelligence.* Implementing change requires gathering information, verifying information, making the case for change, and winning buy-in from key constituencies. That's not necessarily easy, and it all requires a certain strategic openness that is very difficult to train. The kind of intelligence I'm talking about typically only comes about as the result of ongoing experience in dealing with prospects and customers.

7. *A large number of appointments leads to a smaller number of prospects; that base of prospects leads to a smaller number of sales.* Your sales come from your prospects. If you take a realistic view of what a prospect is, and hold yourself to a strict quota of active prospects at all times, you will be successful. The trick is to recognize that we lose prospects at times when it doesn't seem like that's what's happening (for instance, when we make a sale, when too much time passes without action, when changes happen in the prospect's world that we don't hear about). The best salespeople compensate for this way prospects have of evaporating; they spend a significant chunk of their time prospecting for new business so they can maintain their base at its optimum level.

8. *Be sure you verify everything.* Some salespeople don't verify because they're afraid of making a mistake in front of the prospect. Here's the problem with that way of working: If you're never corrected, the odds are that your plan won't make sense to the other person! Remember: The opposite of wrong is right. You want the prospect to right whatever you've gotten wrong. That means that when the prospect corrects you, you win!

9. *To win long-term commitment, you must know what's really going on in the account, and the best way to do that is to ask repeatedly for short-term action in the relationship.* Your aim is always to find out what level of commitment really exists with any given contact, and how that commitment reflects your likelihood of moving forward in the relationship with that person. The surest way to determine whether commitment exists is to ask specifically and in an impossible-to-ignore way for some kind of action from the other person.

FROM THE FRONT LINES

Finally, here is a last set of great ideas from the front line. They come from great business leaders, and they are worth considering closely before we wrap up. Each, I think, carries important implications for your sales career:

- "Stressing output is the key to improving productivity—while looking to increase activity can result in just the opposite." —Andrew Grove

- "We are all manufacturers: Making good, making trouble, or making excuses." —H.V. Adolt

- "Above all, we wish to avoid having a dissatisfied customer. We consider our customers a part of our organization, and we want them to feel free to make any criticism they see fit in regard to our merchandise or service. Sell practical, tested merchandise at reasonable profit, treat your customers like human beings, and they will always come back." —L. L. Bean

- "The question is, then, do we try to make things easy on ourselves or do we try to make things easy on our customers, whoever they may be?" —Erwin Frand

- "Do not fear mistakes. You will know failure. Continue to reach out." —Harold S. Geneen

- "Show me the businessman or institution not guided by sentiment and service—by the idea that `he profits most who serves best'—and I will show you a man or an outfit that is dead or dying." —B.F. Harris

- "The consumer isn't a moron. She is your wife." —David Ogilvy

- "Deals are my art form. Other people paint beautifully on canvas or write wonderful poetry. I like making deals, preferably big deals. That's how I get my kicks." —Donald Trump

POINT TO PONDER

I'd love to hear about how the principles in this book have worked for you. Please e-mail me at contactus@dei-sales.com to share your thoughts and ideas.

Good luck!

APPENDIX A

Seventeen Keys to Getting More Appointments

*L*et's take a minute to look at the universe of people to whom we're trying to sell. We can separate them into three distinct categories.

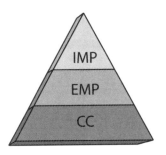

IMPs are people who are already in the marketplace. These are people who are actively looking for your product or service. If you were to ask these people, "What do you need?", they would give you an exact answer because they have already determined that they do in fact "need" something they have not yet obtained. They're actively searching. As you can see, this is a relatively small group.

EMPs are people who are entering the marketplace. These people have made a similar decision, but there is not the same sense of urgency as there is with the IMP group. They typically say "We're looking" or "We're comparing." This is not a very large group, either.

The third group is the biggest. It consists of people who are presently outside our marketplace. We call them cloistered customers, or CCs. They already have a relationship with some vendor. We generally have to contact CCs ourselves. This larger group is where we want to go for growth—by helping them do what they are trying to do better. But we have to make more of an effort when it comes to making the case for change. And we have to understand that they're probably not going to call us.

The IMP and EMP groups are too small for us to be able to count on them for continued sales. We must constantly reach out to people in the remaining group to build our base of prospects and customers. The best way to do that is by making cold calls.

Here are 17 keys to launching an effective cold calling campaign that targets cloistered customers:

1. Build your schedule around a brief daily calling routine. Make the calls each and every day. Don't fall into the trap of postponing cold calls until you "run out of prospects." Prospect consistently, as part of your daily selling routine. If you wait until you notice that you have no business on the horizon, you will experience stressful up-and-down patterns in your income.

Never forget: Rejections equal dollars. Prospecting work drives the entire sales cycle. Every rejection you receive during your daily cold calling sessions is worth cold, hard cash to you. Think about what that means for a moment. Every single "no" you hear as a result of one of your cold calls means that you're one step closer to getting a high-quality prospect into your selling system. And keeping the system full at all times is the name of the game.

Bouncing between good months and bad months eats up your time, energy, and attention. You can bring about more stable, more predictable, more efficient, and more lucrative levels of performance by keeping your prospect base full at all times. Recognize that the rejections themselves are worth money to you because they, and they alone, are what get you closer to the high-quality prospects you must have.

The bottom line: Prospecting every day allows you to channel energy you would otherwise spend on panicking into more productive sales work.

2. Ask directly for the appointment. Check out one of our online courses (at www.dei-sales.com) or attend a D.E.I. Management Group training session in appointment making. By doing this, you'll master the structure of the call, and you'll be sure to build your call around when the appointment will take place, not whether it will take place.

Don't ask, "What's a better time for you, Tuesday morning or Wednesday afternoon?" Instead, ask, "Can we get together Tuesday morning at 10:00?"

Your calling script must feature a reason for the call and a benefit statement that will capture the listener's attention. Ask for the commitment. Say the person's name; briefly explain who you are, what you do, and how your company has benefited others. Then ask directly and without apology for a face-to-face meeting.

Asking for the appointment in this way is a little like throwing out a ball to someone. The person you throw the ball to has to react somehow. Will he or she toss the ball back to you? There's only one way to find out. Throw the ball in the first place!

Which is better? To throw out the ball and notice exactly what happens next? Or not to throw out the ball and imagine that the other person is interested in playing ball with you when he isn't?

3. Make two attempts. During cold calls, make two attempts to set the appointment, then move on to the next call. Do not engage in lengthy debates with the person. If you cannot schedule the appointment by making two direct, polite attempts to meet at a specific date and time, conclude the call and dial someone else.

If you frequently find yourself in arguments with people you are cold calling, you should change your approach. Build an outline that you can follow, stick to it, and disengage from negative exchanges.

Have you ever seen a gerbil? It's a cute little animal that has an engaging, but unproductive, way of going around in circles. You must have seen a gerbil in action. It makes its way onto the little metal wheel and runs for all it's worth. The problem is, it never goes anywhere. Salespeople who constantly engage in long, pointless disputes with the people they cold call remind me a lot of gerbils. They run for all they're worth, but they never, ever get anywhere during these impassioned exchanges. Don't be a gerbil. Make two polite requests to set the appointment by proposing a specific date and time. If you don't get anywhere, disengage tactfully and move on to your next call.

4. Take control of extended conversations. Conversations in which the person says, "That sounds interesting, tell me more," can be quite tricky. Do not get drawn into a long conversation. Briefly respond to the person's query or issue, and then immediately return to your request for the appointment.

We have monitored thousands of cold calls over the years. A cold call that exceeds a few minutes in length is statistically unlikely to yield an appointment. Long calls mean one of two things: either the call turned negative or the person is trying to screen you out and avoid scheduling a face-to-face meeting by posing "knockout questions."

Your numbers will improve if you politely but firmly take control of long conversations and return to the topic at hand—whether or not it makes sense to get together Tuesday at 10:00 AM.

Try this the next time you get caught in an extended conversation:

> *Prospect:* "This is fascinating. What kind of pricing would you offer for someone who wanted a service contract on a Humminah Humminah 3700 unit?"
>
> *You:* (Instead of a long, drawn-out answer that may not match this person's situation): "Well, for that kind of contract, we'd typically be looking at pricing between X and Y."

(Without pausing, immediately follow up with a question of your own.)

> *You:* "I'm just curious, why did you choose the 3700 unit?"
>
> *Prospect:* (Gives any answer.)
>
> *You:* "You know, that's really why we ought to get together. We've worked with a lot of people who chose the 3700 for that reason. I'd really love to get together with you so I can tell you about some of the work we've done. How's Tuesday at 10:00?"

5. Track your numbers. Know how many dials it takes you to get someone to pick up the phone for a completed call. Know how many completed calls it takes you to generate a discussion with a decision maker. Know how many discussions it takes you to schedule an appointment. Know how many of your scheduled appointments actually turn into face-to-face visits. Know how many visits you must go on before you make a sale.

Track your numbers every day and monitor them constantly! Track your activity in these categories each and every day:

- Dials

- Completed calls

- Appointments

- Visits

- Sales

6. Practice. Practice your cold calling approach until you could deliver it authoritatively when roused from a deep sleep. Develop a script that works for you and stick with it.

One great way to practice is to deliver your call into a tape recorder, listen to it, and then note where you can improve your delivery. Practice your approach until you develop a confident, purposeful tone. If the words of your script say, "We should get together," but your tone of voice says, "I would rather be doing anything on earth than calling you," you will not set a lot of appointments!

Write down the words of your calling approach. Practice them until you can deliver them naturally and confidently. Track down a tape recorder, take it to a quiet place, and set aside half an hour of uninterrupted time. Then deliver your cold call approach into the machine. Rewind it and play it back.

Most of us don't like the sound of our own voice when we hear it reproduced electronically. Listen to the tape anyway—at least twice. The first time, you'll begin to get used to the tone, patterns, rhythms, and cadences of your own delivery. The second time you listen to your tape, take written notes about what areas you should try to improve.

Even veteran salespeople who have been using the telephone as part of their sales routine for years are often startled to learn, upon listening to recordings of their practice sessions, that there are major areas for improvement. Ask yourself: Is my delivery too fast or too slow? Do I place unnecessary emphasis on certain words? Is my tone confident, purposeful, and professional? Am I varying my tone?

7. Remember the point of the call. The point of the call is to set the appointment. Nothing more and nothing less. Unless you are selling within a telemarketing environment (that is, one where you're supposed to close during a call), it is a huge mistake to try to sell over the phone.

8. Always leave a message. Always leave a message, either with a human being or on a voice mail system. For tracking purposes, consider a message to be the equivalent of a discussion with the person you're contacting. (See Key 13, which concerns the frequency of your calls to individual contacts.)

Messages are often better mediums for contact than direct conversations with the contact. Use this message format for voice mail systems (assume ABC Company is a company with which you currently do business that the contact will recognize).

"Hi, Ms. Smith. This is Randi Jones from Acme Widget. I'm calling you regarding ABC Company. Please give me a call back at 212-555-1212."

Keep your messages short!

9. Schedule calling time flexibly. Each industry you target is different. Each company you call is unique. Maintain flexibility in scheduling your cold calls so you have the very best chance of connecting with various groups of decision makers. Experiment with your schedule; monitor results from your calling periods so that you take advantage of the best times to contact people.

10. Never vent at anyone. Resist the temptation to "blow off steam." Even if you're completely frustrated with the results of your calling efforts—or with anything else in your life!—be a professional. Keep your tone friendly, approachable, and calm at all times.

You can get yourself —and your company—in serious trouble by blowing off steam at a receptionist, decision maker, or other representative of the target company. Don't do it—ever!

11. Follow the "four cold" rule. Make no more than four cold attempts to contact a decision maker at a particular company during a given month. This is a vitally important principle that is ignored by the vast majority of salespeople.

Don't be one of those salespeople who say they've made 20 cold calls when they've called two contacts ten times each. Call each new contact you want to reach no more than four times over the course of a month.

Don't call leads too often

Don't call the same lead over and over again during the week. There are three big reasons to avoid doing this:

1. You waste your own time. Each repeat call you make represents time and energy you could be spending more intelligently by reaching out to a new contact.

2. People don't appreciate being pestered.

3. You may be tempted to count each repeat call as a separate cold call, which it isn't! We've had people complain to us in training that they've made hundreds of calls without being able to generate a single appointment. In such situations, it always emerges that the person is counting repeat calls as new calls. In other words, he or she is calling the same 20 people—ten times a week each!

If you make hundreds of calls, be sure you're actually connecting with hundreds of different organizations. Count only new cold calls to brand-new opportunities when you track your numbers. Only call any individual contact once a week.

12. Beware of "friendly" calls. Having actually reached a decision maker, make no more than three attempts over the course of a month to connect with that person to set up an appointment. Don't make calls for the sake of friendly—but unproductive—conversations. If three calls after your initial "good call" with a contact are not enough to get this person to meet with you, it is time to move on to someone else.

If you can't get a Next Step, consider the contact an inactive lead and call him or her no more than four times in a calendar month. (See Key 11.)

Beware of "great conversations." One of the traps we can fall into is that of calling up someone we know is not going to set up a meeting with us and wasting time having a "great conversation" with that person. If the discussion does not yield a Next Step for you, it is not a great conversation!

There really are people who love to spend half an hour (or longer!) chatting with a salesperson, but who have no intention whatsoever of actually working with that salesperson. Who knows why this happens? Maybe your contact is bored with the workday, or lonely, or deliberately trying to irritate the boss. It doesn't really matter why some people talk your ear off without any intention of buying from you. They do!

By following this rule, you'll avoid wasting your precious time "connecting" with people who have no intention of moving forward in the sales process with you. Make only three "warm" attempts to set an appointment with a given contact over the course of a month.

13. No extended phone tag. Phone tag destroys your numbers. Play no more than three rounds of phone tag! After the third round, call the person's assistant or secretary and say, "Mr. Brown and I have been playing phone tag for quite a while. All I'd really like to do is set an appointment for 3 PM on Tuesday. Is he available then?"

A certain amount of phone tag is inevitable, given the reliance on voice mail systems in today's business world. However, if you never make any attempt to put a halt to the "you just missed him" syndrome, you will spend most of your time trying to return messages, and less time than you should actually setting appointments. Your numbers will suffer.

Don't let that happen. Contact the person's assistant or secretary directly after the third round of phone tag and suggest a specific date and time for an appointment.

14. Never ask, "Is this a good time?" If you ask the person you call, "Is this a good time?" you will get a predictable response: "No, I'm actually pretty busy right now." Don't ask if it's a good time. Don't ask if it's a bad time. Say the person's name, identify yourself, briefly state why you're calling, and then ask directly and specifically for the appointment.

People respond in kind. You influence the other person's response by the subjects you decide to raise during the call because people respond in kind. If you decide to make the subject of the conversation "whether or not this is a bad time," the person you call will respond in kind. Thus, when you ask, "Is this a bad time?" you will often hear, "Yes, actually this is a really bad time."

If you decide to make the subject of the conversation "whether or not you're interested in making a million dollars," the person you call will respond in kind. When you ask, "Would you like to learn how to make a million dollars?" you will often hear in response, "No, I'm really not interested in learning what you have to say about making a million dollars."

If you decide to make the subject of the conversation "when we can get together," the person you call will respond in kind. If you say, "Can we get together Tuesday at 3:00?" you will often hear in response, "Well, Tuesday's full. What about Wednesday?"

15. Be direct and specific when you make your follow-up calls. Suppose you call Mr. Jones on January 1st to set up an appointment. Suppose he tells you, "I'm much too busy now, call me back on February 1st." When you call on February 1st, what should you say?

Here's the most direct—and the best—approach:

"Hi, Mr. Jones. This is Joan Smith from Acme Widget. When we spoke back on January 1st, you said I should call you today to set up an appointment. How's next Tuesday at 1:00?"

If the person has questions about the nature of your meeting, answer them briefly, then politely but firmly return to the topic at hand. That topic is (you guessed it) whether or not the person will meet with you next Tuesday at 1:00.

16. Follow the yes, rather than waiting to hear the word no. Someone who works for us made a number of prospecting calls over the course of a ten-week period:

- He made 293 calls to different organizations.

- He reached decision makers at about half of them. He wrote the rest off as no answers (whether or not they said the word no), and set up 49 first appointments with the remainder.

- He ended up going on a total of 83 visits (that's first appointments plus follow-up appointments).

- He closed 10 new sales, which met his goal of a sale a week for that time period.

Not proceeding to the Next Step is a form of saying no. Think again about the example you just read. Of the 293 businesses the salesperson called, only 10 bought, but he had to talk to—and get past!—the 293 to reach the 10! The trick is to know when the person has said no (for now, so you can move on to the next person.

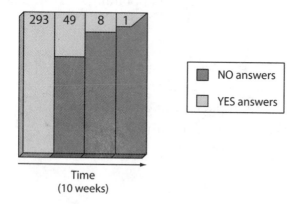

Time
(10 weeks)

Here's what the person's ten-week performance chart probably would have looked like if he'd spent the whole period talking
to people who had refused to give him a Next Step . . . but who had
never actually told him to stop calling. Notice the difference!

By choosing instead to follow the yes answers, instead of
waiting to hear the word no, he hit his income goal. You can take
the same approach—and get the same result. Keep piling up the no
answers, and keep following the yes answers as far as they go.

17. Keep learning. Don't stop here. Make a commitment to
ongoing professional development. Learn all you can about improving your selling cycle in general, and about boosting your
phone prospecting numbers in particular.

A poll of high-achieving salespeople found that the vast
majority made some regular investment in their own professional development over time. This is a particularly important
point because many companies provide no training or ongoing
support for salespeople interested in career growth.

To learn more about training in appointment making from
D.E.I. Management Group, call 800-224-2140.

APPENDIX B

Some Thoughts on Telesales

*T*here are all kinds of ways of selling over the phone. Sometimes people gather all these different ways of selling under a single heading: telemarketing.

As I see it, though, telemarketing describes only a very narrow segment of the various ways salespeople use the telephone to close sales. Let's look briefly at the different types of selling over the phone.

TELEMARKETING

What I call telemarketing is, essentially, the call that interrupts my dinner.

This is the person who calls prospects (often consumers at home) and recites a pitch (usually long) that's meant to secure a purchase commitment (usually during a single call). They don't have an easy job.

These people are caught between a rock and a hard place. They're subjected to resistance and abuse from the people they call; many consumers resent their monotone, low-information selling approach. But changing that approach is often difficult.

Typically, telemarketers are forced by their employers to recite a prewritten script word-for-word, a script designed to be used by literally hundreds of other telemarketers. There's often little or no room for innovation, or for connecting effectively with individual prospects.

Most telemarketers are asked to act as a human direct mail piece. That's really what it boils down to, isn't it? Their job description is to call people and deliver a prewritten speech verbatim, without any attempt to make what they say sound human, and without any attempt to interact with the other person on the line. They say the pitch a dozen, or a hundred, or a thousand times, and wait to see who buys. A friend of mine used to sell over the phone as a telemarketer; his manager told him to deliver his script verbatim, no matter what the other person said. If there was ever an interruption, the salesperson was supposed to say, "I understand how you feel," and then pick up from exactly where he had left off. Not a great way to build a relationship!

This kind of selling is extremely inefficient and is pretty much a waste of time for everyone involved, including the salesperson. If you've got this kind of job, and if you don't have any leeway whatsoever to gather information from your prospect, the best advice I can give you is to keep your eye out for new career opportunities!

SINGLE-CALL TELESALES

This is the label I give to people who sell over the phone, but who don't have to wear the same kind of "straitjacket" that telemarketers do. In other words, they have a little bit of discretion and can develop some rapport and gather meaningful information over the phone.

This is a relatively simple sale that takes place over the phone, and may extend to two or more calls. The seller could be calling a prospect or a current customer. In the case of the call to the customer, the seller is likely to simply introduce himself or herself, and then follow up by saying. "I noticed that you've already bought X; we have a special on Y this month."

I call this kind of selling *by the way* selling. It's often based on a phone call in which the seller has an initial exchange with the prospect or customer, then says, "By the way, you may also be interested in . . ."

These people generally have a very good list to call (better, for instance, than the lists that telemarketers typically work with). They don't barrage their prospects and customers with massive scripts. They have brief calls, many of which turn into good sales conversations. They rarely, if ever, make follow-up calls to the people they contact.

MULTIPLE-CALL TELESALES

People who sell in this environment must initiate the relationship over the phone, gather information from a prospect or current customer, develop a customized proposal, and follow up by phone. The sales cycle extends over a number of calls, typically somewhere between two and six.

This kind of selling typically does not require in-depth presentation skills or the ability to build relationships with many contacts within a prospect organization. It is usually based on identifying a single decision maker, having a few "good calls" with that decision maker, developing a customized proposal (written or verbal), and then asking for the business.

COMPLEX TELESALES

These people have a complex selling cycle that is almost identical to those of salespeople who meet their prospects and customers in person (known as field reps). The sales cycle just happens to play itself out over the phone—and, not infrequently, via fax, e-mail, or Web conferences.

These salespeople are often responsible for selling high-ticket technical goods and services (such as software and Web design services). They often have to develop relationships with multiple contacts within a buying organization. They do all of their selling in a "virtual" environment, and rarely even meet their prospects and customers face to face. Their contacts may be spread out over a very large geographical area.

This sale almost always plays out over a series of calls. Information-gathering skills are essential to success for people working in a complex telesales environment.

INCOMING TELESALES

Some telesales professionals work in an incoming environment, meaning the customer or prospect calls in, often as the result of a direct mail piece, catalogue, infomercial, or other promotion.

This kind of sale often involves an unexpected overlap in customer service issues. The salesperson may have to handle not only sales inquiries as a result of a marketing effort, but also phone calls from people who receive the wrong merchandise. By the same token, these salespeople may find themselves talking to customers who want to have the kind of conversation they would normally have with a really good counter person at a retail store.

Unfortunately, salespeople who receive inbound calls don't always get the training they need to deal effectively with these kinds of service-related calls.

IMPROVING PERFORMANCE IN THE TELESALES ENVIRONMENT

The advice that follows applies to everyone who works in the telesales environment except the telemarketer. (Sometimes I think the best strategy for telemarketers would simply be to call during the day, rather than during the evening, and leave lots of brief, effective phone messages. You'd get a high percentage of good discussions with the people who called back!)

For everyone other than telemarketers, the outbound sale has certain common elements:

- I make a call and find out something about you.

- I send you something, either an order or an e-mail or catalog.

- I set up the Next Step.

- I suggest something that you could buy that you don't know about already.

Inbound telesales professionals go through essentially the same steps, but they must first qualify that there is real interest. The best way to do this is by finding out what made the other person decide to call in the first place. This way, inbound telesales staff can find out if the person is actively in the marketplace, is just entering the marketplace, or is already a customer of somebody else.

So there's a common structure to the relationship. That having been said, there are certain things we have to compensate for in today's telesales environment.

Basically, the people we call have been called so often, by so many poorly trained salespeople, that they've been conditioned to assume that they are about to speak to a moron. They expect to receive a monotone delivery and poor questioning skills. Because people have been trained to expect these things, when we are making calls, we have to instantly a) create rapport and build credibility and b) identify, early on in the relationship, exactly what level of interest might exist.

Here's how we trained people to do that recently. We were working with a group who got incoming calls; this group of salespeople worked at the qualified ad section of a major metropolitan newspaper. Typically, people would call them up and say, "How much is the smallest ad that could run in the paper?"

We trained the salespeople to answer that question briefly ("It ranges between X and Y") and then immediately ask questions: "What is it you're trying to sell? How long have you been trying to sell your motorcycle?"

We trained them to listen to the answer that came back, and ask an appropriate follow-up question: "How have you been trying to sell it?" After a few of these exchanges, the salesperson we trained would say something like this: "You know what? I've got a great idea. Why don't you just try a box and put a border around it; that way we might be able to get you a little bit higher visibility and see if we can get the item sold for you." By asking a few simple questions and then making a recommendation, the salespeople were establishing rapport, building credibility, and qualifying the prospect—that is, verifying that interest in working together did exist. Sales rose dramatically.

The same basic principles apply to the outbound call, but there's the added challenge in those calls that the person we're calling is going to have some kind of negative response for us. ("I'm not interested," for example.) We are interrupting the other person, and we have to be ready for a negative response. The point of our approach, or script, in the outbound call is simply to get that negative reaction out on the table so we can turn it around and then ask a meaningful question that will help us establish rapport, build credibility, and qualify the prospect. (For instance: "You know what? That's exactly what ABC Company said when I called them, and now they're one of our best customers. Just out of curiosity, what are you doing right now to safeguard your company's data?")

With outbound telesales, the trick is to be so well prepared with your turnaround that you can instantly and smoothly move into that all-important first question. Once you've done that, your chances of engaging in an actual conversation increase. With a little practice, you'll find that people react well to this turnaround-leads-to-a-question technique—in part because they're so used to having telemarketers deliver long speeches and ask narrowly-focused yes-or-no questions that sound like they were drafted by a prosecuting attorney.

To learn more about developing effective telesales strategies, visit D.E.I. Management Group's Web site at <www.dei-sales.com>, or call 1-800-224-2140.

A P P E N D I X   C

Ideas for Your Next Step Strategy

*B*efore you go on an initial meeting with a prospect, you must have a plan in mind for how you will end the meeting. In most cases, your objective will simply be to secure another appointment by supplying a reason to get together again with the prospect for a second or subsequent time.

What are the Next Step strategies you will use at the end of your next meeting? Here are six of the most effective ways to return to the prospect:

1. *Present an outline.* Schedule a time to show the prospect a short written document that gives an overview of how your company's products/services can help the prospect meet his or her goals. You might say, "Let's get together next Monday at 2:00 so I can show you an outline that will give you an idea of what our plan for you might look like."

2. *Meet with an expert/resources/manager.* Bringing in a product expert, a company resource, or your manager is a great way not only to advance, but to escalate, the sale. You might say, "Let's set up a meeting for next Tuesday at 2:00 so I can introduce you to our technical people."

3. *Meet with a happy customer.* Have your prospect talk to or, better yet, meet with a happy customer. These contacts can provide a great third-party endorsement. You might say, "Let's get together with Mark Ryford of ABC Company for lunch next week. How's Wednesday at 1:00?"

4. *Give product/service demonstration.* Illustrate how your product or service works. This can help you to continue information gathering, and also show the prospect how he or she could benefit by using what you have to offer. You might say, "What I'd like to do is come back here next Thursday at 3:00 to show you how the model we're talking about would work. How does that sound?"

5. *Go on tour.* Ask to go on a tour of the prospect's company if this is relevant to the implementation of your products/services. You might say, "Can you and I take a tour of the plant next week so I can see where the equipment would actually be used? How's Monday at 2:00?"

6. *Give an invitation.* Inviting a prospect to be a guest at a company-sponsored event, training program, or similar gathering will enable your contact to see your operation and meet key people. This is a great way to continue building momentum in the relationship. You might say, "I'd like to invite you to a free seminar my company is sponsoring. It's taking place this Friday at 9:00 in the morning. Can you make it?"

APPENDIX D

Six Effective Negotiation Tactics

In virtually any negotiation setting, both sides share some similar interests. The challenge is finding out what those interests are! Here are six effective strategies for determining the other side's interests and negotiating more effectively:

1. *Ask, "Why?"* Examine the position the other party is taking and ask yourself why he or she is taking that stance. You might want to ask the other person, "What's your basic concern in wanting XYZ to happen?" Also, ask yourself, "Why have they not made that decision yet? What are the issues that are currently preventing this person from saying yes?" Once you determine what may stand in the way, you can attack the problem.

2. *Realize there may be other influences involved and devise an option for mutual gain.* Every negotiator has a person or group whose opinion he or she values; this could be a boss, client, colleagues, family, or spouse. Broaden the other party's options. Don't search for a single answer to an issue—there is usually a large universe of possible answers to any given situation.

3. *Don't overlook basic human needs like security, control over one's life, and a sense of belonging.* There is always more at stake than money. It is your job to identify such factors and sort them out. When you do, acknowledge that you appreciate the other person's interests. A great way to do this is to say, "As I understand it, your main goal/concern is _____ . Have I understood you correctly? Do you have other important issues for us to discuss?"

4. *Write down the other person's interests as they reveal themselves during the negotiating process.* Doing this will help you to remember the interests, improve the quality of your assessment, and improve the quality of your interaction with the other person. People appreciate communicating with someone who demonstrates a willingness to take notes about their most important interests and goals.

5. *Before entering into any negotiation situation, identify the point at which you are willing to walk away.* Answer this question: If this negotiating session does not work out well, what is my fall-back position? Remind yourself during the negotiating process that the best deal is sometimes no deal at all. Constantly review the point at which you will walk away, and if the negotiation does not point toward a better agreement than that, walk.

6. *Remember that prospecting continuously is your very best negotiating strategy.* In other words, if you have sufficient prospects in your system, you have more options and you can more confidently make the choice to walk away if the terms under discussion do not meet your minimum requirements. Never forget: Your sales process and your negotiation strategy should be intimately related!

I N D E X

ABOUT THE AUTHOR

*S*tephan Schiffman, a self-made millionaire, is the founder and president of D.E.I. Management Group, Inc. and has been America's premier sales and motivational trainer since 1979. He is a Certified Management Consultant and has trained more than 450,000 people worldwide. Mr. Schiffman is the author of a number of successful sales and marketing books, including *Cold Calling Techniques (That Really Work!)* and *Getting to "Closed."* He lives and works in New York City.

WHO IS D.E.I. MANAGEMENT GROUP?

D.E.I. MANAGEMENT GROUP, INC., founded in 1979 by Stephan Schiffman, has long been recognized as one of the nation's premier companies in delivering sales training programs and revenue solutions for organizations ranging from *Fortune* 500 companies to start-ups.

D.E.I. uses face-to-face training and distance learning programs to help organizations do what they do better by posting
measurable improvements in team skill sets in:

- Appointment making

- Prospect management

- High-efficiency selling skills

- Telesales

- Integrated sales coaching

- Negotiating

- Multichannel selling.

To date, D.E.I. has trained over half a million salespeople in
North America, Europe, South America, and the Pacific Rim at
companies such as ExxonMobil, Nextel Communications, Boise
Cascade, GE Capital, CompUSA, DataMonitor, Fleet Bank,
Keyspan Energy, Microsoft Canada, SunAmerica, AT&T Net-
works, and EMC^2.

Key concepts D.E.I. trains include:

- The objective of each step is to get to the Next Step.

- The definition of selling is helping people do what they do
  better.

- No one "needs" us or what we have to offer; if anyone did
  "need" us, they would have already called us.

- Our number one competitor is the status quo—what the
  person or organization is already doing.

- Sell to the obvious by asking how and why the person is already doing what he or she is doing.

- The sales process is an extended conversation; we can control the flow of that conversation.

- The longer a sale takes out of its normal sales cycle, the less likely it is to happen.

- The key to effective sales is ratios, not numbers.

- All responses we hear are in kind; all can be anticipated; all are likely to be told in stories.

- 75 percent of the work in the ideal sales process occurs prior to the proposal or presentation of your plan.

- Our close should be a natural outgrowth of the sales process that sounds like this: "Makes sense to me. What do you think?"

- We want the prospect to decide to buy; we don't want to have to sell to the prospect.

- We can predict future income based on current activity.

To learn more, visit <www.dei-sales.com> or call 800-224-2140.

Bulk Pricing Information

For special discounts on
20 or more copies of
Sales Don't Just Happen
call Dearborn Trade Special Sales
at 800-621-9621, extension 4307
or e-mail tjoseph@dearborn.com.
You'll receive great service
and top discounts.

For added visibility, please
consider our custom cover service,
which highlights your firm's name
and logo on the cover.
We are also an excellent resource
for dynamic and
knowledgable speakers.

Dearborn™
Trade Publishing
A **Kaplan Professional** Company